Praise for
When Faith Catches Fire

"*When Faith Catches Fire* is both an exploration and a celebration of the 'salsafication' of the church—God's work among Latinos and Hispanics in the United States and worldwide. This topic is prophetic and indispensable."

—JOHN ORTBERG, senior pastor of Menlo Church
and author of *All the Places to Go*

"The growing Latino presence is widely recognized as a critical theme in the contemporary United States. But as Rodriguez and Crosby show so powerfully, that presence has a powerful and transformative religious dimension. *When Faith Catches Fire* is a timely and inspiring survey of the vibrant world of Latin faith. An exciting book!"

—DR. PHILIP JENKINS, distinguished professor of history,
Institute for Studies of Religion, Baylor University

"*When Faith Catches Fire* is the prophetic and unapologetic response to the passionate wave of change that is on the cusp of exploding from the church to the corridors of Washington. Rodriguez and Crosby have unearthed the undeniable sound of the forthcoming Latino era. It's the dawn of a new day, and Latinos are leading the way."

—SERGIO DE LA MORA, founding lead pastor of Cornerstone
Church in San Diego and author of *The Heart Revolution*

"In *When Faith Catches Fire,* Samuel and Robert bring us up close to this incredible growing movement of Latino Christians. Read it, and you will find your own faith enriched and reignited."

—ROMA DOWNEY, producer, actress, and president
and chief content officer of Lightworkers Media

"The Hispanic and Latino church is on fire! I recommend the reading of this book if you are looking to serve and serve well in the midst of our twenty-first century multicultural society."

—DR. SAMUEL PAGAN, dean for Hispanic programs,
Jerusalem Center for Biblical Studies

"This carefully researched, balanced, and highly readable book provides a superb overview of one of the most important developments in the religion and culture of our times. The section on what a vigorous Argentine pope means for Latin American protestants is a jewel of clarity. The volume will be indispensable for leaders and laity alike in all denominations."

—DR. HARVEY COX, Hollis professor of divinity emeritus,
Harvard University, and author of *The Market as God*

"Samuel Rodriguez and Robert Crosby provide a much-needed perspective on the global church. . . . Readers will be inspired to live out a more passionate and joy-filled faith, focused less on the rules of religion and more on cultivating a soulful relationship with their Creator and those in their community."

—BOBBY GRUENEWALD, founder of YouVersion, the Bible App

"For many, the Latino Reformation is unknown, unrecognized, and unimportant—three good reasons why every white and black Christian needs to read *When Faith Catches Fire*."

—DR. SCOT MCKNIGHT, Julius R. Mantey professor
of New Testament, Northern Seminary

"*When Faith Catches Fire* is a faithfully documented work which reflects the growing influence of the Latino people in the United States and the positive effects it has had upon this nation."

—REV. ALBERTO M. DELGADO, MA, THD, president
of South Florida Hispanic Ministers Association

"The passionate fire from the heart of this book will serve as a rallying cry to all Latinos and beyond. Now is the time we must unify in the gospel of Jesus Christ and reach this world for Christ."

—Dr. Ronnie Floyd, senior pastor of Cross Church
and past president of the Southern Baptist Convention

"Samuel Rodriguez and Robert Crosby masterfully submerge us into the enthusiasm, passion, and hope of the Latino church."

—Guillermo Aguayo, co-founder of *Salvemos a la Familia*
("Save the Family"), Lima, Peru

"Truly, God is at work today and the Hispanic and Latino church has caught fire. Rodriguez and Crosby have captured this divine work in a remarkable way in *When Faith Catches Fire.* These younger leaders and scholars have encapsulated the genuine key to living, uniting, and changing the world . . . *with passion!*"

—Dr. Robert E. Cooley, president emeritus,
Gordon-Conwell Theological Seminary

"*When Faith Catches Fire* shines an informed light on Latinos among us, a multiethnic population of Christian faith shaping the future of the American church."

—Dr. Mark DeYmaz, pastor of Mosaic Church in central
Arkansas and president of Mosaix Global Network

"In *When Faith Catches Fire,* the authors educate the reader on the flourishing Latino church in America and give us imagination for what's possible when the church is less segregated, more multicultural, and embraces the beauty of different cultures."

—Gabe Lyons, founder of Q-Ideas and author of *Good Faith,*
unChristian, and *The Next Christians*

WHEN FAITH
CATCHES FIRE

Other Books by Samuel Rodriguez

Are You a Third Day Christian?:
Move Beyond Revival Into the Fullness of God

Be Light: Shining God's Beauty, Truth,
and Hope into a Darkened World

Path of Miracles: The Seven Life-Changing Principles
That Lead to Purpose and Fulfillment

The Lamb's Agenda: Why Jesus Is Calling You
to a Life of Righteousness and Justice

Other Books by Robert Crosby

Living Life from the Soul: How a Man Unleashes
God's Power from the Inside Out

More Than a Savior: When Jesus Calls You Friend

More Than Rules; It's a Relationship: Getting from Guilt to God

The One Jesus Loves: Grace Is Unconditionally Given,
Intimacy Must Be Relentlessly Pursued

The Teaming Church: Ministry in the Age of Collaboration

The Will of a Man and the Way of a Woman:
Balancing and Blending Better Together

WHEN FAITH CATCHES FIRE

EMBRACING THE SPIRITUAL PASSION OF THE LATINO REFORMATION

SAMUEL RODRIGUEZ
& DR. ROBERT CROSBY

Foreword by Robert Morris

WATERBROOK

To Dr. Jesse Miranda and Dr. J. Don George:

Two servants of God committed to a church that is both multiethnic and multigenerational. We honor you as our exemplars, and we ask for a double portion of your passion for God and his people.

———

Do not forsake me, O God,
till I declare your power to the next generation,
your might to all who are to come.

—Psalm 71:18

I remind you to fan into flame the gift of God, which is in you.

—2 Timothy 1:6

CONTENTS

FOREWORD

For many years it's been on my heart to see the church come together. In fact, I think that's what heaven will look like—all nations and ethnicities worshiping God together as one, just as it was prophesied in Revelation 7:9–10. However, many of us have issues of the heart that only God knows about and only God can heal. Our prejudices and pride isolate us and divide the body of Christ. It can happen to all of us. In fact, it happened to me.

When my daughter, Elaine, was three years old, she was playing with a friend of a different race. As I watched them play, the Lord spoke to my heart and asked, *Is it all right with you if your daughter marries someone of a different ethnicity?* I thought about that question and quickly responded in my heart, *Of course, Lord! If he loves God and loves Elaine and is a man of character and integrity, it's fine.* Then the Lord said, *No, that's not what I asked. I asked if it is all right with you.*

I knew what God was saying to me. In essence it was, "Robert, you have some issues in your heart because of the way you were raised and where you grew up. Racial prejudices and beliefs were imparted to you that you didn't even know about, and I want to deal with it all." In the following days and weeks, God started opening my eyes and changing my heart.

And that's exactly what I hope this book will do for you. As you read *When Faith Catches Fire,* I believe you'll be deeply affected and your eyes will be opened to something phenomenal God is doing today in the Latino church. The Spirit of God is igniting the faith and influence of Hispanic Christians and churches all over the world and right here in our communities.

One of the most exciting things about *When Faith Catches Fire* is that it's a collaborative project written by Samuel, who is Hispanic, and Robert, who is white. These two dynamic leaders have joined together to help shine a light on something God is doing among us. You'll be inspired and challenged by their personal stories and great insights.

The Latino Reformation is not only a blessing; it is a gift to us and an opportunity that pastors, church leaders, and Christians everywhere should embrace. God is using it to reignite our passion for him. It's one thing to have faith; it's another thing to see that faith catch fire! And that's exactly what's happening with Hispanic believers. The passion they have for God stirs me deeply, and I hope it spreads to churches across our nation.

To this day, God continues to grow my heart and deepen my love for people of all ethnicities and backgrounds. The end of my personal story is that my daughter ultimately married a wonderful young man who loves the Lord with all of his heart and loves my daughter. He is a man of character and integrity, and he is African American. Can I tell you we now have some of the most beautiful and wonderful grandchildren you have ever seen? We absolutely do!

I'm so thankful God dealt with things in my heart that I didn't even know were there. As you read this book, will you ask him to open your heart and give you the eyes to see so he can do the same for you?

ROBERT MORRIS
Founding Senior Pastor, Gateway Church, Dallas/Fort Worth, Texas
Best-selling author of *The Blessed Life*, *The God I Never Knew*, *Truly Free*, and *Frequency*

Those Salsafied Christians!

Embracing a More Passionate Faith

> One consequence of the growing Latinization of
> American society is the increasing Pentecostalization
> of American Christianity.
>
> —Dr. Luis E. Lugo, director, Pew Research
> Center's Forum on Religion and Public Life

There is something about a fire, something so compelling about a flame, something that catches our attention and makes us want to stop whatever we are doing and draw closer. Whether blazing amid logs under a living-room mantel or encircled by stones at a campsite, a fire quickly becomes the hearth, and heart, of a family or a community. There is a magnetic attraction. It keeps people warm, illuminates their interactions, and becomes a focal point that brings people together.

And fire is an ideal metaphor for passion, a burning and consuming force that is unquenchable. It is also a fitting image for faith. When belief moves from mere mental assent to a deep, convictional belief, it does something powerful. *Faith catches fire.*

Latino Christians are catching the fire. In many ways they are changing their world today, and in the past five years, they have changed mine (Robert's)! In fact, Latino Evangelicals, "up from 14 percent in 2006 to 18 percent in 2013," are the "fastest-growing religious group in the country."[1] There is just something about their faith in God and the ways so many of them experience it, practice it, embrace it, and live it that I find absolutely compelling. There is a passion burning in the souls of so many Latino Christians today, blazing trails of local, regional, national, and global change. The jury is no longer out on this. The tipping point has hit. In the next few years (and decades), their influence will continue to grow and be felt in the church, in business, in government and politics, in the economy, in arts and sports, and in the important and pressing arena of race relations.

If the white Euro-American church has led the way in stewarding the last millennium, then quite possibly the Hispanic church is being called on to rise up and steward the next one. If the white church has filled the practical role of the global Elijah for the past several decades, serving as prophet-leader, then she now needs to recognize that a new Elisha (that is, the Latino church) has been busy working in the fields and is ready to bear a mantle of responsibility, an anointing of ministry, and servant-leadership for days to come.

The change isn't coming.

It's here.

We are convinced a major change is upon us. But far too many churches, pastors, Christians, leaders, government officials, and others have not yet acknowledged what is growing up all around them. That is one of the main reasons we have joined together to write this book.

Reformation

As this book releases, this very year we celebrate the five-hundredth anniversary of the Protestant Reformation. At that critical point in history, an uncertain monk with a certain fire burning within challenged man-made misconceptions that were fueling ministerial malpractices of all sorts and relegating the Word of God to popes, priests, and prelates. Martin Luther unsuspectingly sounded the clarion call of reform to a church much in need of it.

Today we are watching a different type of "reformation" occur. A few years ago, I (Samuel) was interviewed by Elizabeth Dias, a reporter for *Time* magazine, on the phenomenal growth of the Latino church. As we pored over multiple statistics and stories on the growth of this movement, I suggested to her that this represents "a Latino Reformation." Her eventual cover article concurred: "What I discovered signaled a Latino Reformation."

The Latino Reformation is in full swing.[2]

Our prayer is that this book will bring awareness and inspire action. As you read it—we urge you to really *read* it, *fully read* it—you will find something much more than just interesting or informative insights. You will realize there is something compelling and dynamic going on all around us, something not to be missed.

A soul moment.

God is blessing the Latino church in the United States and across the world in incredible ways. One of the most notable ways is the spiritual passion that seems to characterize so much of Latino spirituality, faith, community, service, and worship.

While much of America and the rest of the world focus on an immigration *problem,* the church should and must focus on an immigration *opportunity.* While government officials squabble over what it takes to become a citizen of our nation, Christians have an opportunity to welcome hundreds of thousands of souls as citizens of the Kingdom of God. While politicians are arguing their opinions, church leaders need to be busy serving and winning souls of every color and background and to find ways to welcome them into their churches, their homes, and their hearts.

Catching the Fire

Latino Christians are the most open and passionate souls I (Robert) know or have ever known. In the past five years, my wife, Pamela, and I have been amazed to see the soul-full faith lived in the lives of so many Latino Christians, from Los Angeles, California, to Lima, Peru. God is doing something special among this group, and the rest of the church needs to see and embrace it.

No one in recent years has challenged me or taught me more about growing my soul than Latino Christians, and one of those I most respect is my co-author on this book, Samuel Rodriguez. Latino Christians have become to my wife and me such an encouragement and example of passionate, wholehearted, open-souled, and on-fire Christianity.

From my connecting with Hispanic pastors and churches in the United States to enjoying fellowship and ministry together with brothers and sisters in Peru, Ecuador, Spain, Argentina, and Chile, there is just something about Latino passion for God, for one another, and for the Kingdom of God that is compelling. Added to that are my friendship and interactions with Samuel and my respect for the work he and the National Hispanic Christian Leadership Conference (NHCLC) are doing around the world.

After overseeing a merger in 2014 of NHCLC and Conela (a Latin America–based organization that serves Latin churches across the world), Samuel now leads the organization. Collectively it is estimated that this coalition represents around five hundred thousand churches worldwide. This is one of the largest networks of believers anywhere. Also, earlier this year Samuel had the honor of becoming the first Evangelical Latino ever to participate in a swearing-in ceremony of a US president. When asked about the invitation to be a part of this event, Samuel said, "The opportunity to speak on the quintessential political platform in the world, and to be able to lift up Jesus on that stage before that global audience, without a doubt is one of the greatest privileges I have ever received in my life." He added, "It's a God-graced opportunity that one cannot turn down."[3]

Here Is the Church

The face of global Christianity is changing. More than we know, the change is happening in our heads, hearts, and hands. Do you remember reciting this as a child?

Here is the church.
Here is the steeple.
Open the doors, and
See all the people!

This two-handed, rhyming childhood ritual tapped our earliest imaginations about the church. Testing more than our dexterity, this rhyming exercise formed ideas and expectations in our minds about where, how, and with whom we worship.

In my young mind at that time, I (Robert) pictured the church as a building whose architecture pointed toward heaven and opened up to reveal a place teeming with people, really wiggly people, and to be really honest, at that point for me—really wiggly white people. My understanding of church has evolved and expanded since my childhood. While our faith is forever tethered to the person of Jesus and our essential beliefs, I now understand that, throughout history, it has experienced both sweeping and subtle adjustments of form and function in order to reach an ever-changing world. As Heraclitus of Ephesus, the famed Greek philosopher, once said, "Everything changes and nothing stands still."

Samuel and I decided to write this book for a few key reasons: (1) we believe the most staggering and significant demographic change facing the church today is the phenomenal growth of the Latino church in North America, South America, and other parts of the world with an infectious passionate faith; (2) we are convinced that much of the non-Hispanic church in the United States and other parts of the world is unaware of this significant development; and (3) we want to make sure that as many Christians as possible are "making the most of every opportunity" for the gospel and especially the ones the Latino Reformation presents to us now (Ephesians 5:16).

The Latino Reformation is impacting the nature of all the church in worship, politics, and servanthood. Not only are these changes occurring in multiple cities, communities, regions, and nations, the potential of more impact is sitting latent in the lives and hearts of many Latinos yet waiting to be welcomed, affirmed, and encouraged by open souls, both ours and yours.

A Not-to-Be-Missed Moment

The United States Census Bureau projects that between 2014 and 2060, the US population will increase from 319 million to 417 million.[4] "By 2030, one in five Americans is projected to be 65 and over; by 2044, more than half of all Americans are projected to belong to a minority group."[5] You read that correctly: *more than half,* which means that the current minorities will become the new majority. That will make America a majority-minority nation.

Dorothy, we are not in Kansas anymore.

We believe the church's greatest opportunities are now multiethnic and multigenerational and that open souls will take the lead. Whether you're a neighbor, pastor, teacher, government leader, or businessperson who wants to reach out to Latinos, this is the book to help you do so, to help you understand more of the significance and immediacy of the opportunity. The wise will do so out of their insight, but all leaders should do so nonetheless, if only for their own survivability. This book holds ideas and approaches that will help. Our hope is that it may become a de facto manifesto for the Latino Reformation movement as well as a quintessential clarion call and wake-up call to evangelistic and discipleship action.

A Lit-Up Church

The church is awakening. It is waking up to its prophetic mandate to be light in the midst of darkness. The Latino church stands poised to light a passionate fuel. The Latino church may be one of the most lit-up churches in the twenty-first century. It is being placed on a stand and shining as never before. The Latino church is no longer following behind and begging for crumbs. By the grace of God, it is leading growth, outreach, and healing among much of the global church today.

And, as mentioned, we believe the Latino church is the new Elisha. First Kings 19:19–21 is taking place before our eyes: in effect, the Latino church has been breaking ground with the ecclesial plow for many decades. However, the Latino church has now grown tremendously and developed compelling skills and graces. She is rising to the needs of the hour. She is also looking for partnering churches, pastors, leaders, and others to become *Latinos del corazón* (that is, "Latinos of the heart"). These open-souled people will be used to open doors for the Latino Reformation to rise in their communities.

The changes are happening all around us, so rapidly that it is staggering. But they are also occurring and emerging so naturally that you could easily miss them. Are you ready for it? Are you catching the fire and passion of the Latino Reformation, or are you, your family, your church, and your community missing it? Will you live with an open soul or a closed one?

A Faith Fiesta!

Experiencing a passionate and celebratory faith is one of the major characteristics of Latinos and the Latino church today. Dr. Samuel Pagan, an elder scholar in the Latino Reformation movement, says that for Latino Evangelicals, "Faith is a fiesta!"[6] He cites Revelation 7:9–12, in which the Bible prophesies a time of people "from every nation and tribe" (Revelation 7:9, NLT) standing together before God's throne and celebrating.

The segregated, bland, faith "line drawings" that existed for many years around the world are changing. God is pulling out his most vivid and diverse palette and adding color to it all. For the openhearted Christian and the willing pastor, God is ready to transform churches from a monochromatic, monolithic presentation of Christendom to a multiethnic, kingdom-culture, colorful presentation that has power and incorporates and reconciles the three elements of passion, purpose, and promise. As a result, a more soulful Christianity is emerging, one that fills the heart, feeds the mind, and fires up the faith.

With all the racial tension we have seen reemerging around the nation and the world, I (Samuel) believe the Latino church can serve as the bridge, as the antidote to much of the racial tension right now between the African American community and the Anglo community, particularly in the areas of race relations, faith relations, and even law enforcement. In a real sense, we believe that God wants to use the "brown" to help unite the "black" and the "white" in America today. In this book, we will show and address some of the ways that it is already happening and can happen.

Not Really a Race

Latinos are not a race. This is confirmed in a Pew Research report that notes, "Federal policy defines 'Hispanic' not as a race, but as an ethnicity." However, the same Pew study notes that 67 percent of Hispanic adults surveyed said that "Hispanic" to them is a race (11 percent) or both a race and an ethnic background (56 percent).[7]

The term *Hispanic* was first used in the 1980 census,[8] but Hispanics can be of almost any race. Also, they come from and live in many nations. Thus, Hispanics have a view of race that is quite different than many other groups in the United States.[9]

"The Latino community in the United States is diverse and includes more than twenty-two nationalities, though in many locales it can and does take on particular national and/or regional identities. This rich diversity has made it difficult to find a suitable umbrella term to describe it. In general, Latinos born in the United States refer to themselves as 'Americans' or by their country of origin (for example, 'Mexican American'). Similarly, Latino immigrants refer to themselves almost exclusively by their country of origin or by the umbrella term given to them by the larger Euro-American society—Hispanic or Latino."[10]

A 2012 study by the Pew Research Center's Hispanic Trends group notes that 51 percent of Latinos have no preference between the terms *Hispanic* and *Latino.* Thirty-three percent still prefer *Hispanic,* which is more traditional. Fourteen percent now prefer *Latino.*[11]

Latinos are a conglomerate, a convergence of black and Anglo and Asian. What brings them together is the language and not the color of their skin, because it is the language component and the cultural threads that derive out of the Spaniard or the Spanish collective experience. For Latinos, language matters. Words matter. Juana Bordas notes that "Spanish . . . is spoken in twenty-two countries and is the language spoken by most people in the Western Hemisphere."[12]

That language of Latinos is passionate and very metaphorical, very poetic. While the American world and the Anglo world are more Geoffrey Chaucer and *The Canterbury Tales,* the Latino world is Miguel de Cervantes and *Don Quixote.* In the Quixote world what you have is a perpetual metaphor, where everything is seen through the eyes of a metaphor and the lens of God's creation, with picturesque applications and allusions. The Anglo world thinks more in linear, sequential, anal-retentive, logical ways or in more of a bland representation.

One of the ways Latinos will be a bridge is through their language.

A Growth Explosion

I (Robert) am excited to see how God is raising up leaders today in the Latino church. It is quite clear to me that Samuel is one of those leaders at the epicenter of the Latino Reformation. It is in his blood, in his DNA. He carries a mantle of leadership responsibility in this movement and is a protégé of some of the most respected elders in it.

After a few months of exposure to the Latino church community (actually, communities, as there are so many of them), my wife and I noticed it was much more than the doctrines or church-development methods of Latinos that were getting into our hearts and minds and making an impression. More so it was their passion and strong sense of community that captivated our souls and transformed our view of the church: a more vibrant, bold, and engaging church.

Our travels to various parts of South America and among Latino Christians and churches in the United States have without exception always left us with one major feeling: *not wanting to leave*! Exposure to these faith communities in various parts of the world consistently serves to fire up our faith. For a couple of years, we tried to describe what we were seeing and experiencing in the Hispanic church that we were too often missing in the white church ethos or culture. We searched for an adjective or two and we fell short. Some of the words we now use include

- personable
- powerful
- engaging
- community oriented
- family (*familia*)
- alive
- welcoming
- magnanimous, a great word that needs to be rediscovered in the church and in the world today

We searched for a fresh, vibrant term to describe what happens to people impacted by this passionate experience of the Latino Reformation. We wanted a spicy and even fiery term that would say it well.

Some of the things we have appreciated the most in our observations have been

- a familial and extremely *welcoming sense of community* that draws you right in and leaves you finding yourself not wanting to leave

- a deep conviction, almost a simple assumption, that the only way to experience power in your life and ministry is by *engaging deeply in practices of prayer*
- practices of *joy-infused singing and worship*
- a passion in *preaching the gospel that is underscored by a sense of prophetic* immediacy and urgency
- a powerful but natural *merging of evangelism and compassion,* of help and of hope, of giving people the gospel and the kind assistance of a good neighbor

Latino Christians have purpose, passion, and promise. One of the benefits of a more soulful (soul-full) Christianity is its holistic approach: it is both vertical and horizontal. In contrast, non-soulful (soul-less) Christianity is either predominantly vertical *or* horizontal. Soul-full faith is vertical, which means we look up to God and it's about God and his kingdom, and soul-full faith is horizontal, which means it's about our families and communities.

So we sought for the word, and we believe we found one: *salsafied.*

Latino Christians in the United States, Latin America, Spain, and other parts of the world are experiencing and practicing a more salsafied, or a fiery and passionate, faith and life. That's it. Once the word emerged, it just stuck with us. And while we believe it is a form of biblical Christianity being practiced and enjoyed by many Latinos, I also believe that through demographic changes, people movement, immigration, and influence, God wants a more passionate faith in the lives of non-Hispanic believers as well.

Open the Doors

As little children we were playfully instructed to put our two little hands together and say,

Here is the church.
Here is the steeple.

Now that we're adults, let's take those same hands and reach out to Latinos in our communities and in our churches, businesses, organizations, homes, and hearts, and remember to . . .

Open the doors, and
See . . .

Not just a handful of wiggly white little fingers but a palette of colors, including the brown, the white, and the black.

Open the doors, and
See . . .

Not just some, but

All the people!

PART ONE

Living with Passion

Loving God with All Your Soul

1

A Soul Moment

The Latino Protestant boom is transforming
American religious practices and politics.
—Elizabeth Dias, *Time*

Sergio de la Mora was twelve years old when he was described as the best skateboarder in Santa Barbara, California. Today he pastors one of the fastest-growing churches in the United States. But his journey involved some deep challenges.

"My brothers used to take me in their low riders to the skateboard parks, and the cultural tension was there," de la Mora recalls. "Here was a young skateboarder getting dropped off as his brothers were part of a gang." He wanted to reject gang life, and he hoped to ride his skateboard away from it.

When Sergio started junior high school, however, he gave in and became a gang member. He gave up his dream of skateboarding out of that life, he recalls, "simply because of peer pressure." At age thirteen, he got into drugs more heavily, and after a gang fight was hospitalized when a rival stabbed him in the back.

When Sergio got out of the hospital, his father took him on a walk through a cemetery. He said, "Sergio, what do you see?"

Sergio said, "Dead people."

Then his father asked, "When did they die?" Sergio reminded him that this information was engraved on their tombstones.

"No, they didn't," his father answered. "A lot of these people died before they got here. If you don't have a vision for your life, you're gonna already be dead."

Not long after, Sergio found a tract about a church. He attended a service, heard the gospel, and became a follower of Christ. He now pastors Cornerstone Church, one of the fastest-growing churches in the United States. From the moment of Sergio's conversion, his faith caught fire, and the light of that growing flame is now impacting thousands.[1]

Transformational

We live in a transformational moment, and the Latino church is uniquely poised to engage it. Old things are fading faster than ever before. New things are emerging. The faithful and nimble will seize the moment. The unfaithful and reluctant will most likely completely miss it.

> Do not remember the former things,
> Nor consider the things of old.
> Behold, I will do a new thing,
> Now it shall spring forth;
> Shall you not know it? (Isaiah 43:18–19, NKJV)

At one and the same time, as a nation and world, we are facing great divisions and yet great opportunities to unite; we live amid age-old contrasting cultures and worldviews that can push us all apart, and yet current technological and collaborative tools can bring us together. Arguably, never in history have we possessed more ways to come together, and ironically, neither have we possessed so many things that can separate us.

Management consultant and educator Peter Drucker more than twenty years ago noted the changes of an epochal era such as we find ourselves in today. He discerned and defined such a moment in time this way:

Every few hundred years in Western history, there occurs a sharp transformation. . . . Within a few short decades, society rearranges itself—its worldview; its basic values; its social and political structure; its arts; its key institutions. Fifty years later, there is a new world. And the people born then cannot even imagine the world in which their grandparents lived and into which their own parents were born.

We are currently living through just such a transformation.[2]

Drucker's words strike a poignant ring in our minds and hearts. We see such sweeping changes occurring around us today locally, nationally, and globally. We are living in such a moment.

The time we are living in is a moment because the Latino population in the United States is rapidly growing. Consider these metrics of change:

- Of the US population growth between July 1, 2013, and July 1, 2014, almost half of the 2.5 million people were Hispanic.[3]
- The Hispanic population in the United States has increased from 12.5 percent of the total population in 2000 to 17.6 percent in 2015.[4]
- In New Mexico, Hispanics represent almost half of the population.[5]
- In California, Hispanics are 39 percent of the population.[6]
- "The Latino population in the United States grew by 43 percent in the last decade."[7]
- By 2050 one in three Americans will be Hispanic.[8]

It is a moment because Christianity is rapidly growing and changing among Latinos and around the world.

- "The center of Christianity has shifted from Europe to the global South [that is, Latin America, Africa, and developing parts of Asia including the Middle East]. . . . In 1980, more Christians were found in the global South than the North for the first time in 1,000 years."[9]

- "Today, the Christian community in Latin America and Africa, alone, accounts for 1 billion people."[10]
- The massive Christian population in Latin America is becoming much more Pentecostal or Charismatic. "In Brazil, for example, the Assemblies of God has 10 million to 12 million members, while the American Assemblies of God church has 2 million to 3 million. So now, the Brazilian church is the big brother and the United States is seen as mission territory."[11]
- "Today, Brazil not only has more Catholics than any other country, but also more Pentecostals."[12]
- The newly elected mayor of Rio de Janiero, Marcelo Crivella, is a Pentecostal-Evangelical. The *Washington Times* reported his astounding election this way: "In this city renowned for bacchanalian excess and tiny bikinis, the election of a conservative evangelical bishop as mayor stands out as yet another surprise in a year of global electoral earthquakes."[13]
- "A century ago, 80 percent [of Christians] lived in North America and Europe, compared with just 40 percent today."[14]
- Pentecostals comprised "5 percent of Christians in 1970," but "today one of four Christians is Pentecostal or Charismatic."[15]

It is a moment because Christianity is not dying! However, it is rapidly growing, shifting, and changing among Latinos and around the world.

- "In 1970, 41.3% of all Christians were from Africa, Asia, or Latin America. By 2020, this figure is expected to be 64.7%."[16]
- In Brazil, "Protestants and Independents combined represented 12.9% of the population in 1970 but are expected to grow to 28.8% by 2020."[17]
- Pentecostal and Charismatic believers "in Latin America have experienced astounding growth, from 12.8 million in 1970 to 181.3 in 2010 and an expected 203.0 million by 2020."[18]

- "Pentecostals [in Latin America] are gaining an increased role in public life. Guatemala has recently had two Pentecostal presidents, and a Pentecostal political party has been founded in Nicaragua."[19]
- "Millennials are the most racially diverse generation in American history. . . . Some 43% of Millennial adults are non-white."[20]

It is also a moment because the largest Assemblies of God church in America is a predominantly Latino church in Chicago.

A Latino "Reformation"?

Although Catholicism was first brought to the Western hemisphere by boat all the way from Spain, the largest Catholic nations as of 2010 are actually Brazil, Mexico, the Philippines, the United States, Italy, and Colombia.[21] The global church has grown much more Latino in the past century. Elizabeth Dias reported, "The Catholic Church has also enjoyed a 500-year monopoly on the region. Latin America, unlike Europe, never had a Protestant Reformation. Thus, Christianity was almost entirely synonymous with" Roman Catholicism.[22] The region had no Martin Luther or John Calvin, until, perhaps, now. Today, the leader of the Catholic Church for the first time ever is a Latino: Pope Francis.

Dias explains that "Catholics comprised 81% of Latin America's population in 1996, and Protestants made up only 4%." She adds, "By 2010, Protestants had jumped to 13% of the population while Catholics dropped to 70%." Samuel told her, "We are in the first generation of the Hispanic Protestant Reformation, and that reformation has taken place primarily via the conduit of the Pentecostal charismatic movement." [23]

But how will this Latino Reformation continue to affect the United States, Latin America, and the world? The passionate faith of these believers is so strong that in many parts of Latin America the Catholic Church is now copying some of the practices, worship forms, and approaches of its sister Pentecostal churches. In some ways and places we are observing the Pentecostalization of Catholicism.

I (Samuel) sincerely believe that we are the first generation of the Latino Protestant Reformation. You can see it all around us. Predominantly Catholic Latin America, for instance, did not truly experience the impact of the sixteenth-century European Protestant Reformation until the 1970s and 80s. This was primarily through the influence of evangelistic, Pentecostal television, missionary efforts, and radio programs.

Is It Really a Reformation?

But is it accurate to call this movement and growth among Latino Christians a *Reformation*? Alberto Delgado, founding pastor of Alpha & Omega Church, a megachurch in Miami, agrees with the concept of a Latino Reformation. He said, "A reformation is to *re*form something that has lost its form. This is occurring among Latinos. This is a new season. The growth and change going on among Latino Christians could even serve to connect other groups together—whites, African Americans, Asians and Latinos."[24]

Not everyone, however, agrees that *Reformation* is the most appropriate term for what is going on among Latino Christians. "I like the term *awakening* more than *reformation* in this case," says Albert Reyes, president of Buckner International. "What we are seeing is something Philip Jenkins spotted early on and wrote about in his book *The Next Christendom*. He noted that the majority of the Church's growth is in the Global South."[25]

"It is a 'reformation', yes," says Dr. Samuel Pagan, dean of Hispanic Studies at the Jerusalem Center for Biblical Studies. "But perhaps it is more of a 'counter-reformation.'" All in all, Pagan warns against overly generalized and grandiose views and versions of the role of the Latino Reformation. He stresses something else, citing that, at best, we all can hope to simply make "a modest contribution" to the work of God in the world today. He notes that this is "because the Kingdom of God is big and our work, by comparison, is small."[26]

"Latinos are turning not just to Protestantism but to its evangelical strain. . . . More than 35% of Hispanics in America call themselves born-again, according to the Pew Forum, and 9 out of 10 of evangelicós say a spiritual search drove their conversion. 'People are looking for a real experience with God,' says [pastor Heber] Paredes. That direct experience comes largely from exploring the Bible. 'We do the best to preach with the Bible open. When they read the Bible, they find a lot of things they didn't know before. They may have had religion, but they did not have an experience.'"[27]

Parenthetically, this is our Latino Reformation. What does that mean? It took four hundred years for Martin Luther's reformation to saturate Latin America. The past fifty years really reflect the beginning of our reformation. Therefore, we have yet to see the fullness of Latino Evangelical growth in America and abroad. But it is happening now right before our eyes.

Something Underlined

From time to time in church history, God seems to underline certain aspects of faith in order to bring a course correction to his people. When we go all the way back to the major and minor prophets of the Old Testament, we see that God's love for his people was so faithful and determined that when they fell into seasons of complacency or disobedience, he refused to remain silent. He sent prophets among them to convey and sometimes display his heart and Word to them. Amid the Dark Ages, the Reformation emerged, and God underlined the role of the Word of God in the life of the church and the individual Christ-follower (that is, Luther's *sola scriptura*).

Now the predominant growth of the church is shifting to the global south. The world and the church are starting to wake up to this tectonic event. The shift numerically and proportionately is stunning. Yet what might God be underlining for the global church amid all of this? What might he be saying to us in all of this? In a word, we believe it is *passion,* spiritual passion: a passion for God and for loving God, a passion for Jesus and for the fullness of his Spirit in our lives, and a passion for people and for loving people.

Latinos are catching and communicating *passion* in fresh and empowering ways. They are engaging a more *soulful* Christianity than most. Of this, we are convinced. We believe in the *Imago Dei,* or the "image of God," and the *Missio Dei,* or the "mission of God," but we also believe God is underlining something else today for his church: the *Passio Dei,* or "the passion of God." The passionate writer of Hebrews said, "Our God is a consuming *fire* (12:29, ESV)."

"Nuestro Dios es fuego consumidor"!

Tozer Nailed It!

One Christian pastor and writer who early on saw the danger of a diminishing passion in the church was A. W. Tozer. In 1948, he summed it up this way:

> Current evangelicalism has . . . laid the altar and divided the sacrifice
> into parts, but now seems satisfied to count the stones and rearrange
> the pieces with never a care that there is not *a sign of fire* upon the top
> of lofty Mount Carmel. But God be thanked that there are a few who
> care. They are those who, while they love the altar and delight in the
> sacrifice, are yet unable to reconcile themselves to the continued *absence
> of fire.*[28] (emphasis added)

As a follower of Jesus, has your soul been truly ignited? Has your faith caught fire?

Through no fewer than three sweeping movements of the past 250 years, God has sought to raise and to rouse his people with a deeper passion. Although each of these epochal movements in the church is unique, they all have one thing in common: *passion.*

Three Sweeping Movements and Moments

While the Reformation of 1517 brought sweeping ecclesial change, in the past few centuries there have also been several stirrings or movements within the church. In the Western Hemisphere these have included, but not been limited to, the following.

The Evangelical Movement

During the transformative revivals of the First and Second Great Awakenings in America and beyond, God stirred a fresh *passion for the lost* in his people. Through great leaders and voices such as Wesley, Whitefield, Edwards, Finney, and others, great passion emerged for a heartfelt response to the gospel of Jesus Christ.

The Pentecostal Movement

From the earliest days of the twentieth century and the fires of Azusa Street, many Christ-followers became freshly and deeply aware of the work of the Holy Spirit. Great movements of prayer, healing, and evangelism evidenced this across the world. God stirred a *passion for the Spirit* and his presence.

Today we believe something else is occurring among the people of God that will also have a long-standing impact on the global church. *Time* ran a cover story on this phenomenon, identifying it as the "Latino Reformation."[29]

The Latino Reformation

While the Evangelical movement was about renewing the priority of the church, the Pentecostal movement underlined the power available to the church through the Spirit. The Latino Reformation in the United States is about *a people,* a people of God who are emerging with a unique and focused set of passions and values. Some in the movement like to refer to themselves as the *Evangélicos.* We believe that God is raising up the Latino Reformation, in part, to stir up a *passion for unity and justice* in the church, and not a minute too soon.

In the Latino Evangelical movement in the United States, the Evangélicos note they have found a happier experience at their new churches for a few reasons, including the opportunity (1) to engage their faith with personal expressions, events, and festivities that reconnect them to their cultural traditions; (2) to hear messages that inspire hope amid life's hardships; (3) to find pathways as immigrants to serve, grow, and lead in a new land; and (4) to experience a more soulful faith through celebration.[30]

According to Jonathan Calvillo, a researcher at UC–Irvine studying California-based Latino Evangelical congregations,

> There is a lot more flexibility and freedom (than in Catholicism) in terms of starting new churches and leadership roles. You can go from leading a Bible study to being a pastor in less than a year, which creates new pathways for gaining respect and status previously not available to them.[31]

These three movements and moments in the church of the past two hundred and fifty years are signs of God stirring the passion of his people yet again. One is Evangelicalism. Another is Pentecostalism. But today, yet another dynamic has been added to this mix: it is the Latinization or, if you will, the *salsafication* of the church. The explosive growth and emergence of Latino or Hispanic believers is bringing a fresh passion to the face and flavor of the global church.

A Defining Moment

Sergio de la Mora recalls another transformational moment in his life, one that forever changed his approach to ministry. It occurred when "God distinctly told me to stop being the pastor I *wanted* to be and start becoming the pastor the community *needed* me to be." It "changed the course of our church forever."[32]

Becoming the "pastor the community needed" involved changes for de la

Mora, including becoming a multiethnic church, adding a Spanish service, remodeling their church facility to fit the community, moving from a single-site to a multisite campus "crossing state lines and international borders," creating a system to make disciples, and breaking with expendable traditions in order to reach a new generation.[33]

What Too Many Churches Are Missing

There is great cause for concern among churches today. In his book *The American Church in Crisis,* David T. Olson says that despite some optimistic church trends in certain polls, "On any given Sunday, the vast majority of Americans are absent from church. . . . If trends continue, by 2050 the percentage of Americans attending church will be half [of what it was in] 1990."[34] Olson continues,

> In the monoethnic world, Christians, pastors, and churches only had to understand their own culture. Ministering in a homogenous culture is easier, but monoethnic Christianity can gradually become culture-bound. . . .
>
> In the multiethnic world, pastors, churches, and Christians need to operate under the rules of the early church's mission to the Gentiles. . . .
>
> As the power center of [global] Christianity moves south and east, the multiethnic church is becoming the normal and natural picture of the new face of Christianity.[35]

Passio Dei

Sometimes it helps us to just stop and pull the lens out a bit, to consider a sweeping overview of what God has been doing in and through the church. In a sense, the first three centuries after the day of Pentecost and the birth of the church was a moment of truth. Much of the challenge of the church's becoming established was in the area of doctrinal purity, or *orthodoxy*.

By the sixteenth century, the church was so "established" it had become controlled and, in some senses, corrupt. Such a system of corporateness, of a works-based religion, had emerged within the church that nothing short of reform would do. That began in the form of a man named Martin Luther. His confrontations were exacting and impactful. Belief as a matter of the heart had to not only be redefined but also recaptured, along with the good work of making the Word of God accessible to the masses. Also, while the overblown role of the priest was reduced, the priesthood of the believer was underlined and re-formed. This was a moment of faith for the church and the reestablishment of right practices, or *orthopraxy*.

Today we find ourselves at another important moment, a soul moment. Through the phenomenon of the Latino Reformation, God is lighting a fresh fire in the souls of his passionate worshipers and followers. This is a soul moment for the church and the resurrection of *right passions*. There are no less than seven ways the Latino Reformation is changing the world. We will look at each of them in the next chapter.

We know that God is devoted to purifying and preparing the Bride of Christ for Christ himself. This includes *right beliefs, right practices,* and also *right passions.* God is doing today something beautiful and not to be missed. He is restoring a deep passion to his people. He is cultivating a more vibrant faith and a more soulful Christianity for those who are willing.

Right passions for God. Theologians would call it *orthopathy.* But there is another word we like that may make it a bit plainer.

The word?

Salsafication.

The salsafication of the church.

FEED THE FIRE
Questions to Ignite Growth and Change

1. What is it about fire that people find so compelling?

2. What does faith look like when it "catches fire"?

3. What kinds of things help to ignite our faith?

4. Which aspects of Sergio de la Mora's story did you find most interesting?

5. Does this season in time seem transformational? In what ways?

6. What could you, your family, and your church do to make the most of this moment?

7. What aspects of the growth of the Latino church catch your attention?

2

The Salsafication
of the Church

Latino Protestants are more likely to get up and dance
in church than to fall asleep there.
—Elizabeth Dias, *Time*

Even megachurches can plateau. Just ask J. Don George. Founding pastor of
Calvary Church in Irving, Texas, George was frustrated by a church that
had reached an attendance level of thousands in Sunday-morning attendance
and yet for a ten-year period was not able to see attendance change by more
than one hundred worshipers. The church was large, a megachurch, but stag-
nated in growth nonetheless. He recalls, "I was frustrated and confused. For
years, our church hadn't been growing. We'd produced magnificent pageants,
conducted powerful outreaches, and invited the most gifted speakers in the
country to preach in our services. . . . Nothing seemed to get us out of our
stagnant condition."[1]

Many churches reach growth plateaus that become very difficult to sur-
mount. The *Cambridge Dictionary* defines the verb *plateau* as "to reach a level
and stay there." For some it is breaking the one-hundred-attendee marker; for
others it is two hundred or even five hundred. But imagine that you pastor a
church or lead an organization and that you have plateaued at a bit higher number, say two thousand or three thousand. Whether it is fifty or five thousand,

plateauing is still the same. No matter how many or how few, plateauing is a challenging place to be.

In 1995, while George was attending the biannual General Council of the Assemblies of God in Indianapolis, God gave him a transformative insight. The keynote speaker that night was Jerry McCamey, who asked everyone to look around the auditorium, then said, "Look at all the faces here tonight. Do you see many people of color? No, this denomination—this church—is too white!"[2]

George then says, "I thought, *How could I have missed this? Where have I been all these years? What was I thinking?* I answered God with a simple prayer, 'Yes, Sir. When I get home, I'll do something about it.'"[3]

While the church continued to be overwhelmingly populated by white attendees, the zip code in which it existed transformed over a few years into one of the most diverse areas in the United States.

Pastor George began to take intentional steps to make changes. One of the most dramatic was bringing in a Latino worship leader for their Sunday-morning services. After this change was made, growth accelerated considerably.

Calvary Church had an experience that we believe would do many, if not all, churches good to share. It got salsafied, and as a result, it will never be the same. Hearing Pastor George tell the Irving story is nothing short of compelling. He is still a white pastor, but without a doubt he is now a salsafied one and having the time of his life.

A Kaleidoscope

Albert Reyes notes that the Hispanic population in America and other places is such a great opportunity for churches today, regardless of their complexion. "Unfortunately," Reyes says, "many Anglo churches today do not talk about the rapid growth of the Hispanic population and of the Hispanic church. If they invested in them more, their churches would *explode* in growth."[4]

In the Irving example, Pastor George had always preached from the pulpit that Calvary welcomed all people in the area, but he admits that he was not taking the initiative to actually invite them himself nor was he urging others to do the same. He simply waited for them to come, but few ever did.

Ultimately, George came to see that "it's not enough to have God's *heart* for all people. We also need to have his *eyes* to see all people in a community." Eventually he came to see that Hispanics, blacks, and Asians had moved from "their" parts of the city and were integrated throughout the community everywhere, except in churches like the one he was pastoring. He finally determined that would change. Today, Calvary Church in Irving is one of the most diverse congregations in the United States.[5]

When Faith Catches Fire

When faith catches fire, you will see Jesus in a way you never have before. Faith is not only something that gets in your heart; it also gets in your eyes, in the sense that it causes you to see things of faith more fully.

For instance, after Daniel had prayed and fasted for twenty-one days, he had a revelation of the Lord: "His body was like beryl, his face like the appearance of lightning, his eyes like torches of fire, his arms and feet like burnished bronze in color, and the sound of his words like the voice of a multitude" (10:6, NKJV).

Ezekiel was told to go out into the plains because God was going to talk to him: "The glory of the LORD stood there . . . and I fell on my face" (3:23, NKJV).

John the Beloved in exile on the Isle of Patmos saw the Lord in his magnificent splendor, glory, and purity: "His head and hair were white like wool, as white as snow, and His eyes like a flame of fire. His feet were like fine brass, as if refined in a furnace, and His voice as the sound of many waters; He had in His right hand seven stars, out of His mouth went a sharp two-edged sword, and His countenance was like the sun shining in its strength" (Revelation 1:14–16, NKJV).

And what did John do at this sight? The passage makes it clear: "When I saw Him, I fell at His feet as dead. But He laid His right hand on me, saying to me, 'Do not be afraid; I am the First and the Last'" (verse 17, NKJV).

God has always wanted to ignite his people with the fire of his presence so that they will light the world. Did you notice how many of these leaders' experiences with God were fiery and glowing with glory? He wanted to do so with the nation of Israel. Isaiah prophesied that God said, "For Zion's sake I will not keep silent, for Jerusalem's sake I will not remain quiet, till her righteousness shines out like the dawn, her salvation like a blazing torch" (62:1).

Salsa Secrets

Salsas and sauces are universally appealing. Many people groups across the world have their own kind of culinary sauce; some even go so far as to call it their secret sauce. American southerners have their gravy, Italians have their marinara, and Chinese have their soy sauce. But in America, when we think of Latinos and sauce, we automatically think of one thing: *salsa,* a favorite among so many!

Unfortunately, there are many non-Latino Christians today for whom salsa may be about the only aspect of Latino culture they have ever experienced. However, if Taco Bell is the extent of your HIQ (that is, Hispanic intelligence quotient), you are unprepared for some major changes going on in our world and coming rapidly at us in the church. This process is the "salsafication" of the church.

Trust me (Sam), there is zero relationship between Taco Bell and the Latin experience. In fact, Taco Bell is to Latino what Australian rugby is to American baseball. It is just an American concoction attempting to brand a fast-food service via the conduit of a cultural experience, and if the goal was authentic Hispanic food or culture, it has failed miserably (sorry!).

The "spices" God is adding to the global church through the Latino Reformation are neither bland nor mild. In fact, they are spicy blends that perhaps many would not expect. The potency of these spices is not found in any sole spice but in their blended nature; they are not only powerful, but they are often paradoxical.

Juana Bordas says, "Since each batch of salsa is different, it is a good metaphor for Latino diversity."[6] But remember, salsa is also a way of life: the spice, the energy, the vitality, and *gusto*! Salsa is a communal celebration to be shared with *familia* and *amigos*. One bowl with everyone dipping his or her chips in it puts a little gusto into life. Salsa reflects the culture's festive nature so beautifully contained in *gozar la vida*, "to enjoy life, relationships, work, and community."

The God-Flavors

Salsa in many settings is associated with spice. It usually enhances a meal or a fiesta (Spanish for "party") by spicing things up. But if the salsa is old and has lost its zest and spiciness, then no one will want it. Similarly, when our faith gets old and remains unrefreshed, it loses its spice or zest; it becomes unpalatable and undesirable.

Jesus talked about "spiceless" or passionless Christians in this way: "You are the salt of the earth. But if the salt loses its saltiness, how can it be made salty again? It is no longer good for anything, except to be thrown out and trampled by men" (Matthew 5:13).

Salt (a good additive to salsa, by the way) is supposed to add something to the meal, not take away from it. Spiritual "spice" or passion or soulfulness is what helps us live out Paul's urgent directive to "make the teaching about God our Savior attractive" (Titus 2:10). The Greek word for "attractive" used in this verse is *kosmeo,* which means "to enhance," "to ornament," "to adorn," "to prepare," "to dress," and even "to garnish."

Eugene Peterson paraphrases the essence of what Jesus said in Matthew 5:13 this way: "Let me tell you why you are here. You're here to be salt-seasoning that brings out the God-flavors of this earth. If you lose your saltiness, how will people taste godliness? You've lost your usefulness and will end up in the garbage" (MSG). That says it so well. Salsafied Christianity at its best in many places around the world is helping to bring "out the God-flavors of this earth." It can do the same thing in your community or city.

The Sources of the Spice

But just where did this characteristic passion or soulfulness now present in so many Latino believers originate? What contributed to there being such a strong sense of it in diverse Hispanic settings, regions, and nations? Samuel Pagan says there are several things he believes contributed to the sense of passion characteristic of the Latino faith experience today. Among them are several influences, including historical, ancestral, ecclesial, Pentecostal, familial, supernatural, and persevering factors. Let's briefly consider them all.[7]

Salsa Source 1: Historical Roots

"Soul-full or salsafied is the right term to describe the Latino faith experience," says Pagan. He notes that the roots of this soulfulness of Latin Americans go all the way back to the Middle East. In 1492 two major global events happened: (1) Columbus found America and (2) Jews and Islamics were expelled from Spain. When these groups were extradited, there was a need domestically for replacement workers to fill the roles they previously held in the market, and the slave trade in these regions resulted.

The expulsion of Jews and Muslims from Spain by King Ferdinand and Queen Isabella in 1492 was a black mark in history. Some three hundred thousand Jews had to convert to Catholicism or flee Spain. The land they occupied, known as Sefarad, had been a refuge for them. When they refused to convert to Christianity, they were raped, mugged, and murdered as they fled to Italy and northern Africa. Others went to Portugal and faced more persecution or expulsion. Those who stayed were targeted by the Spanish Inquisition. Small groups remained in the Ottoman Empire, which welcomed exiles. However, most descendants of these groups are now in Latin America, Israel, France, or the United States. This displacement played into the sufferings experienced in history by many of those now considered Latino.

There was an intensity in the culture that was shown or manifested in Latin America. Then, once you add the geography of the region, the weather that afforded regular outdoor engagements, and other factors, a resultant passion and enthusiasm developed in the ethos of Latin Americans. But from earlier years for many who eventually migrated, the Middle East influenced much of the culture. In fact, coffee itself is something that originated not with Juan Valdez in Colombia but, rather, in the Middle East (that is, Arab-ica).

Salsa Source 2: Nation-of-Origin Ties

Latinos in the United States maintain close relationships with their families and friends who live in twenty-two Hispanic nations of origin. They are collectively and "culturally linked with people in North, Central, and South America." Historically, since more than one-third of the continental United States was part of Mexico, "these cultural roots remain strong." These connections make the influence of Latinos no less than global. Much of the growth of the Latino population in the United States has been through immigration. It is also important to note that unlike many other immigrants, "Latinos are acculturating, not assimilating. They are bringing their gifts into the mainstream and *infusing the United States with a Latin flavor*" (emphasis added).[8]

Additionally, Latinos who have migrated to Evangelical and Pentecostal home churches find that these faith communities "serve as a 'second family': people with whom they pray, do community service, barbecue and celebrate such milestones as baptisms and quinceañeras [celebrations of fifteenth birthdays]."[9]

Salsa Source 3: Ecclesial Oppression

Not only did some of the Latino passion likely develop while enduring much conflict, warfare, and oppression geopolitically, there were also the religious oppressions they endured. As noted earlier, the Roman Catholic Church often exerted much control upon the people. For many years the Catholic Church and the government worked closely together, and at times they were almost indistinguishable. However, something unique occurred in America in the 1980s that, Pagan notes, seemed to catch the attention of Latin Americans. It happened when Jimmy Carter became America's first outwardly born-again president. This much-celebrated narrative of a national leader emerging with a story of a personal and public Christian faith gave hope to the roles of influence potentially available to emerging Latino Evangelicals: the opportunities to serve and influence their culture. From this point on, the Protestant influence in Latin America rapidly accelerated. Pagan says, "Many left the Catholic Church and moved into the Evangelical and Pentecostal ones."[10]

"Most Hispanics in the United States continue to belong to the Roman Catholic Church. But the Catholic share of the Hispanic population is declining, while rising numbers of Hispanics are Protestant or unaffiliated with any religion. Indeed, nearly one-in-four Hispanic adults (24%) are now *former* Catholics, according to a major, nationwide survey of more than 5,000 Hispanics."[11]

The Pew Forum research confirmed the growing disenchantment with the Catholic Church among Latinos. The report listed in decreasing order of importance the main reasons that Latinos are leaving: they just "drifted away," "stopped believing in the teachings of their childhood religion," "found a congregation that reaches out and helps its members," experienced a "deep personal crisis," moved "to a new community," or married "someone who practices a different faith."[12]

A small number of respondents cited other reasons for moving away from the Church of Rome. These included "particular aspects of Catholicism that they now reject, such as the veneration of saints and the Virgin Mary, or trust in the Catholic priesthood," due in part in light of "the scandal over sexual abuse by clergy."[13]

Salsa Source 4: Pentecostal Appeal

While a culturally shaped Latin passion already existed, the Pentecostal movement came along in these regions and supercharged it.

> From the movement's origins among a few adherents in the Azusa Street Revival in Los Angeles (1906), Pentecostalism grew to some 12 million adherents by 1970, and now incorporates some 600 million worldwide in its various expressions, a fourth of all Christendom. David Barrett's monumental *World Christian Encyclopedia* states that in 1900, only seven-tenths of 1 percent of Christians were Pentecostal; today, approximately 25 percent are.[14]

The growth of Pentecostalism, or what Empowered21[15] refers to as being "Spirit-empowered," has exploded among Latinos. As cited statistically in the last chapter, Pentecostal believers in Latin America have experienced astounding growth, increasing by over 1400 percent in number from 1970 to 2010.[16]

Salsa Source 5: Supernatural Experiences

Most Latino Evangelicals embrace the supernatural.[17] The manifestations of the Holy Spirit and the seeking of the same are frequently on the menu of Latino Christians and churches. Faith to Latino Christians is more than something to reflect upon; faith is also something to powerfully and personally experience and engage boldly.

The Pew Forum studies also noted the frequency of Hispanics citing the supernatural. "Pentecostals are particularly likely to report having received a divine healing (64%) or a direct revelation from God (64%), to have witnessed the devil or spirits being driven out of a person (59%), and to say they have spoken in tongues (49%)."[18]

In light of Pagan's and others' theories of the origins of Latino passion and the primary sources of development, you might say that Latino passion

- *emerged* amid a soul wound that came during a violent time of history
- *fortified* Latinos against religious oppression and in the quest for spiritual freedom
- *erupted* in response to the outpouring of the Holy Spirit
- *grew* in the context of familial and collectivist spiritual communities
- *advanced* aggressively through supernatural events and prophetic ministry

Salsa Source 6: An Overcoming Spirit

Another factor among Latinos that has spiced the salsa in their souls is learning to overcome difficulties, hardships, and obstacles. Juana Bordas describes it well:

> [For Latinos] life can be difficult and, like a roller coaster, it has ups and downs. . . . For immigrants separated from their families, for migrant workers, or for children starting school not knowing English, life can be difficult indeed. . . . Latinos have faced all of these obstacles, but they are still dancing, singing, celebrating, enjoying their families, and having more fiestas than any other group in America.[19]

The book of Revelation actually speaks often of those who overcome. It lists no less than twelve promises reserved for those who would endure. Joy Dawson beautifully describes the path of those who face unexpected fires:

> I believe, as God's children, we're all either in a fiery trial (with varying degrees of heat), heading for one and don't know it, or have been in one

and need more understanding of how to get through the next one more successfully. I believe the degree of the heat of God's fire in each believer's life is proportionate to the extent of God's plan to use each one for the extension of His Kingdom and to bring glory to the name of the Lord Jesus Christ. This is vividly illustrated in the lives of Job, Abraham, Joseph, David, Daniel, Mordecai, Esther, Jeremiah, Mary, Paul, and the apostle John. In each case the intense heat came when they were living righteous lives before God and men.[20]

The Church of Tomorrow?

Recently, I (Robert) was asked to write an article for a church publication on the topic "The Church of Tomorrow." The focus? *What key trends do you see emerging in the church today, and how can we prepare for them?* The following insights were culled from interviews with church leaders around the nation. I conducted and transcribed all of the interviews. After I read through these prayerful prognostications several times, key themes emerged, themes that confirm statistical and demographic changes. Here are the top five themes and trends the study found about the church of tomorrow.

More Diversity—Much More. Leaders noted the undeniable landscape and demographic changes that are substantially altering the field of mission. This is occurring in no minority group more than among Hispanics. According to a *New York Times* report on the census, for the first time in American history, in 2002 Latinos became the largest minority group in the United States, surpassing African Americans.

More "Natural Virtuals." While technological advancements have been wonders for Boomers, Gen Xers, and Millennials to watch unfold, the latest emerging generation (Gen Z or the Homelanders) view them all as commonplace just as their elders saw writing a letter or making a phone call.

The "Bigger Smallers." The rapid growth of the megachurch and attractional-based church forms have created a greater agenda for "smaller batch" craft forms of church that are scalable to the setting and appetite of the disciple. Urban centers will require more scalable shapes and sizes in church ministry. For big churches to be strong churches, they have to nurture the small circles of faith in their midst.

A Greater Pentecostal Presence. Of all the things the global church is currently becoming, it is becoming much more Pentecostal or "Spirit-empowered" in nature. Statistics confirm this.

Evangelism + Compassion. While for decades some expressions of the church focused more on evangelism while other focused on compassion, Millennials and Homelanders are looking for ways to follow Christ by doing both. These responsibilities are no longer going to be seen as separate.

Three of these top-five trends are significantly related and combine to form the motivational nexus for this book.[21] Did you catch them? They are more diversity, a greater Pentecostal presence, and the joining of evangelism and compassion. Each of these factors is powerfully at work in the Latino Reformation going on all around us right now.

A Growing Influence

Barna Group research found that Hispanics are influencing many areas of American society: "From their socially conservative celebration of family and expressions of faith, to their education and vocational pursuits and political preferences, by sheer numbers and demographics Hispanics are shaping societal trends. With four out of five Hispanic Americans identifying themselves as Christians (both Catholic and Protestant), their perspectives are also shaping American Christianity."[22]

This influence, however, goes far beyond the United States. It is global in its reach. Donald Miller and Tetsunao Yamamori cite the rapid growth of the Latino church, especially the Pentecostal varieties. They also characterize Pentecostalism as "a major new social movement" moving "Christianity's center of gravity . . . to the developing world."[23] Pentecostalism arguably thrives amid adversities extant in the world, such as violence, political unrest, and challenging economics.

Now the mission "tables" have turned. As earlier noted, the center of Christianity has moved to the global south. This is widely acknowledged. And now missionaries are actually coming to North America and Europe from those former mission-targeted nations. The sense of where to find the "lost" is changing in our world today.

The Salsafied Church

Salsafication is the "adding of flavor" to the church. Now, we have had that before. We have had that since the turn of the twentieth century with the Asuza Revival, which became the primary impetus not only through men such as William Seymour but also others named Juan Lugo and Francisco Olazabal. These two individuals were the primary conduits through which the Latino world received the Pentecostal message.

The salsafication of the church is the church becoming more Latino. During the past twenty to twenty-five years, we have seen more Anglo and African American churches incorporating Spanish lyrics in their praise and worship, and more Latino pastors and preachers have been invited to speak in their conferences. Salsafication is well underway.

Instead of missing, resisting, or even fearing the emergence of Latinos in the United States and other places, I (Robert) would urge you to become a Latino *del corazón* ("of the heart"). You will find that Latinos are not monolithic, nor can they resist someone who cares enough to be just a little interested and neighborly. The soul salsa in the magnetic Latino community is something the United States and other places sorely need, and I believe it has come to us "for such a time as this" (Esther 4:14).

FEED THE FIRE
Questions to Ignite Growth and Change

1. What factors contribute to the growth of churches (and organizations) hitting a plateau?

2. What is the "salsafication" of the church? Have you experienced it? Explain.

3. What opportunities does salsafication offer churches today?

4. Which of the "salsa sources," the factors contributing to Latino passion, stood out to you? What has contributed to the cultural "salsa" of the Latino experience?

5. In what ways do you see salsafication happening today?

6. Which of the five characteristics of the church of tomorrow are you engaging? Which are you missing?

7. What steps do you and your church or organization need to take to become more multiethnic?

The Third O

Passio Dei

Our God is a consuming fire.
>   —Hebrews 12:29, ESV

The course of your life is determined by the condition
of your heart.
>   —Sergio de la Mora, pastor,
>   Cornerstone Church of San Diego

Paul was the Prince of the Prepositional Phrase. This apostle of the church was passionate and soulful in his faith. He emphasized the heights and the depths of knowing Christ. He described faith as "of" this, "through" that, "in" this, "by" that, "for" this, "beyond that," and on and on. Paul was into depth and more. He would have made a good Latino or a Latino del corazón! Consider these Pauline statements and passionate superlatives:

> Oh, the *depth of* the riches *of* the wisdom and knowledge *of* God!
>   How *unsearchable* his judgments,
>   and his paths beyond tracing out! (Romans 11:33)

> To me, though I am the very least of all the saints, this grace was given, to preach to the Gentiles the *unsearchable riches* of Christ. (Ephesians 3:8, ESV)

> I pray that out of his glorious *riches he may strengthen you with power through his Spirit in your inner being,* so that Christ may dwell in your hearts through faith. And I pray that you, being rooted and established in love, may have power, together with all the saints, to grasp how *wide* and *long* and *high* and *deep* is the love of Christ, and to know this love that surpasses knowledge—that you may be *filled to the measure of all the fullness* of God. (Ephesians 3:16–20)

Paul spent much time developing the church in Ephesus and, at one point in his ministry, seemed to use this location as a base of operations. He underscored the need for their love and passion for God, their depth of intimacy with and experience in God, to be strong and regularly stirred up and renewed.

Practices and Passions

Since the Reformation of the 1500s, the global church has focused much on the development and definitions of her doctrine and practices of faith. This has led to volumes of theological writings and reflections as well as countless sermons, teachings, trainings, resources, seminars, councils, conventions, seminaries, catechisms, etc. In theological terms, the church has focused much, and arguably primarily, on the two Os: orthodoxy and orthopraxy. While orthodoxy is the understanding of *sound doctrines of faith,* orthopraxy, much as it sounds, is about the discipline of *sound practices—the praxis—of faith.*

Much of Christianity has been about these two integral parts of the church and the life of the Christian, orthodoxy and orthopraxy. Thus, we have done much to cultivate the mind, organization, and work of faith, but we often left the soul untended and underdeveloped. Without the enlivenment of the soul and the work of the Spirit, a dry religion seems the best we can muster.

The fact is, religion leaves us wanting. I (Robert) don't even *like* the word anymore. And my frustration is nothing new; many people feel it. As a matter of fact, throughout the centuries many others have also found themselves worn out on religion. Boston's own John Adams, one of America's founding fathers, early in his career considered going into the ministry. As one author writes, Adams changed "his mind when he observe[d] local church services and the fierceness of disagreement so inherent in the religion of the time."[1] He found a great conflict between the complex demands of the church and the simplicity of the gospel. In his own words, he asked the question (1756):

> Where do we find precepts in the Gospel, requiring . . . Convocations, Councils, Decrees, Creeds, Confession, Oaths, Subscriptions and whole Cartloads of other trumpery, that we find religion encumbered with in these days?[2]

Clearly John Adams was worn out on religion in his day. Yet, as his words reveal, it wasn't the gospel (that is, "good news") God had given that turned him off but all the "accessories" (that is, "cartloads of trumpery") men had added to it. Wisely, Adams knew the Scriptures well enough that he could differentiate between the inspirations of God and the perspirations of men, between human notions and divine intention.

However, on the Day of Pentecost the Holy Spirit released a third O, refreshing the souls of men and women. That was when the Spirit struck a passion and broke open the "living water" Jesus promised would flow out of their souls (see John 7:37–39). The third O is ortho*pathy,* the *sound passions of the faith.* We believe God is using the Latino Reformation today to help strike, stir, and rekindle flames of passion in the souls of churches, church leaders, and all Christians. God is calling us to love him with our entire mind, strength, *heart, and soul* (see Mark 12:30; Luke 10:27).

In the twentieth century there was an amazing emphasis on orthodoxy, which I (Sam) have no problem with whatsoever. And then in the latter part of the century, it seemed to pivot more to orthopraxy: how you practice or live out the gospel. All too often today, orthopathy or orthopathos is the neglected third rail in much of the church.

The three Os basically represent a faith that affects the head, the hands, and the heart, the head being orthodoxy—the doctrinal, foundational component of Scripture; the hands being orthopraxy—the practice of Scripture, the practical, day-to-day application of God's Word; and then orthopathy—the affective, emotional, and soulful engagement with God, his Word, and his world. That's the part Latinos enjoy and offer in a big and growing way today.

No Small Scandal

I would argue that historically the white church has really focused on *orthodoxy,* what the Word says; the black church has focused on *orthopraxy,* how you live out the gospel with social justice and equality; and the Latino church is saying, "Yes, but what about *orthopathy*?" We must make room for this. What about engaging the emotional, the affective domain? Not only what it looks like in our daily lives and in our worship services, but more so in a holistic manner that even engages our hearts, our sentiments, our feelings, our passions.

A. W. Tozer referenced John Wesley's comments as he noted a diminishing of passion in the church:

> It is a solemn thing, and no small scandal in the kingdom, to see
> God's children starving while actually seated at the Father's table. The
> truth of Wesley's words is established before our eyes: "Orthodoxy, or
> right opinion, is, at best, a very slender part of religion. Though right
> tempers cannot subsist without right opinions, yet right opinions may
> subsist without right tempers. There may be a right opinion of God
> without either love or one right temper toward Him. Satan is proof of
> this."[3]

So it's the passionate gospel of which we speak—that is, the passion of Christ. Such a powerful gospel cannot be limited simply to right doctrines and practices; it is also given to affect right, and righteous, passions. Just as the eye can see and discern colors, so can the soul feel and discern passions.

A Spotlight on Seven Practices of Soulful Faith

Just what are the characteristics and practices of a soulful Christianity? During hundreds of conversations among Latinos in dozens of states and nations, we found a few common practices clearly discernible and broadly embraced. We have seen these common practices all the way from Los Angeles to Lima, from Barcelona to Belize. While there are many Christian groups who practice some of these, our contention is that an unusual number of Latino Evangelicals and churches practice most or all of them; they are gloriously endemic to the DNA of Evangélicos (a term used by many to refer to Latino Evangelicals) today.

Practice 1: Honoring Christ in Their Lives Daily—¡Honor a Cristo Diariamente!

Many Latino Christians intentionally engage the presence of Jesus Christ in prayer, intimacy, and passionate worship every day. In many places, this is the first part of the day and, in some, at the earliest part of the day. They practice the presence of Jesus in their lives. This practice develops a *worshiping* soul.

Practice 2: Centering Their Lives on the Word of God—¡Se Centran en la Biblia!

At a time in history in which many people have allowed their view and use of the Bible to diminish, Latinos are emphasizing the vital place the Word of God has in the life of a believer. This practice is the foundation of Latino passion and develops a *well-fed* soul. It also fuels a sense of responsibility and a desire to live a life of purity.

Practice 3: Empowered by the Holy Spirit—¡El Poder del Espíritu Santo!

Latino Christians love experiencing a faith in its fullness, in its full enjoyments and expressions. This is experienced through the work of the Holy Spirit in the life of the believer. The fullness of the Spirit grows an *overflowing* soul and is the Source of the passion.

Practice 4: Connected Multiethnically—¡Conectado Multi-Étnicamente!

In several places today, Latino churches are reaching out to other nationalities and ethnicities. They are looking beyond themselves to their neighborhoods and caring for others. These practices help grow a more *loving* soul as we work with someone who shares our passion.

Practice 5: Generationally Linked—¡Generacionalmente Vinculados!

The Evangélicos are incredibly connected to their families. They believe in honoring their husbands, wives, sons, daughters, and all relatives. Dr. Samuel Pagan confesses they are a culture that is "externally patriarchal, but internally very matriarchal."[4] Juana Bordas says, "In our homes we say, 'The man wears the pants in the house, but the woman tells him which pair.'"[5] The place of family, elders, and children plays a vital and deeply felt important role of passing on the passion. Strong family commitments help grow an *honoring* soul.

Practice 6: Community Oriented and Engaged—¡Orientado a la Comunidad!

The GLOBE study, a cultural survey of most nations of the world, shows that predominantly Latino nations and regions are much more collectivist than the United States (which tends to be more individualistic).[6] There is a deep sense of community among Latino churches and faith groups, as well as seeking to unite their passion. Community helps grow a *connected* soul.

Practice 7: Transforming Their World One Soul at a Time— ¡Transformar el Mundo!

There is an "edge" to the ministries and outreaches of Latino Christians that stands out in our world today. This edge is characterized by things bold and prophetic. In using the word *prophetic,* we mean something that is sharply and boldly attuned to the need of the hour or of the moment. This can be felt in Latino preaching, worship, and leadership. The prophetic edge in life, faith, and prayer helps grow a *bold* soul with a passion for the lost, a faith clearly mixed with expectation and hope.

Engaging the Fiesta!

One way to consider the differences of the three Os is in the context of a birthday party. Let's say you receive the birthday invitation telling you that a celebration is scheduled and how (where and when) you can be a part of it. In a sense, that is orthodoxy, receiving the essential information.

Next, let's say you go out and carefully select the right gift to bring to the birthday boy or girl. You put your mind and your hands to work to select and purchase something appropriate to give. That is the orthopraxy, engaging in the work needed to be a blessing at the party.

Then, let's say after receiving the birthday announcement and picking out an appropriate gift, you fail to show up at the party. In a very real sense, you have missed something vital. You have missed the point of it all. Engaging in the party, the fiesta, is the orthopathy; it is the celebration itself. Remember, to the faithful Jesus said, "Enter into the joy of your master" (Matthew 25:21, ESV). Another version says, "Let's celebrate together!" (NLT).

Donald Miller captures this same idea in another way.

> The whole time Jesus was extending an invitation to a spiritual marriage, our oneness with Him allowing God to see us in Christ's righteousness rather than our own. It would be most tragic for a

person to know everything about God, but not God; to know all about the rules of spiritual marriage, but never walk the aisle.[7]

Music and worship are certainly a big part of the ethos and soulful ways of the Latino church and movement today. In an interview with Elizabeth Dias, Samuel described the inclusivity: "The [Latino] evangelical church says this: Listen, you want to come to our church? If you are Mexican, we will show you a church where you can sing mariachi music. If you are Puerto Rican, we will have salsa. If you are Dominican, we will have merengue. If you are Colombian, we will have cumbia."[8]

Fullness

The teachings of Jesus and of Paul and the nature of Christianity itself are all about fullness. We are told in Colossians 2:9 that "in Christ lives all the *fullness* of God in a human body" (NLT). Jesus said, "I have come that they may have life, and have it to the *full*" (John 10:10). Paul wrote to the Ephesian Christians, "I pray . . . that you may be *filled* with all the *fullness* of God (3:18–19, NRSV)."

Christian tradition and theology actually tend to underscore orthodoxy and orthopraxy much more than they do orthopathy. The first two are often tied by theologians to the nature of God and his image. Thus, orthodoxy is connected to the emphasis on the *Imago Dei* ("image of God"), a human description of God's character and nature. Additionally, the *Missio Dei* ("mission of God") is more indicative of orthopraxy. It is focused more on the great work and purpose of God shown in the gospels and in the blessing of Abraham (to become a blessing to the nations of the earth).

This, however, leaves another key component and the third leg of the stool: orthopathy. Perhaps embracing the term *Passio Dei* (the passion of God) would be a good complementary term to adopt and use more often as soulful Christians, even among Pentecostals and Evangelicals. Thus, we are being conformed to the *Imago Dei* (the image of God) shown by our engagements in the *Missio Dei* (the mission of God) and energized by the *Passio Dei* (the passion of God).

The *Imago Dei* is the mark: the image of God.

The *Missio Dei* is the method: the mission of God.

The *Passio Dei* is the motivation: the passion of God.

In his book *The Pursuit of God*, A. W. Tozer underlined the passion of God in a biblical metaphor of fire.

> In fire He appeared at the burning bush; in the pillar of fire He dwelt through all the long wilderness journey. The fire that glowed between the wings of the cherubim in the Holy Place was called the *shekinah*, the presence through the years of Israel's glory. And when the old had given place to the new, He came at Pentecost as a fiery flame and rested upon each disciple.[9] (italics in the original)

The Ferocity of God

God is often associated with fire in the Scripture. Bianca Juarez Olthoff notes that

> throughout the Old and New Testaments, we find that God has *responded* by, *appeared* in the form of, and been *likened* to fire. In every case, fire is viewed as a symbol of God and His ability to radically change our lives.
>
> God made a covenant with Abraham using the symbol of a smoking fire and blazing torch (Gen. 15:16–17).
>
> Through the fire of the burning bush, Moses received a commission and calling (Ex. 3:2).

Fire protected the Children of Israel during the exodus out of slavery and provided light to guide them (Ex. 13:21).

God displayed His holy purity through fire on Mount Sinai (Ex. 19:18).

God revealed His presence through fire to Shadrach, Meshach, and Abednego (Dan. 3:25).

The Holy Spirit transformed and empowered Jesus' followers in the form of fire on the day of Pentecost (Acts 2:3).[10] (italics in the original)

"Our God is a consuming fire" (Hebrews 12:29, ESV).

Faith Catches Fire

God wants every Christian to be in touch with not only the orthodoxy of belief and the orthopraxy but also the orthopathy—the *Passio Dei*. In other words, he wants us to experience faith caught on fire.

- When faith catches fire . . . our beliefs turn into boldness.
- When faith catches fire . . . our desire turns to desperation.
- When faith catches fire . . . our prayers turn into soul cries and intercessions.
- When faith catches fire . . . the written Word of God in our minds becomes the spoken Word of God to our hearts.
- When faith catches fire . . . we move from knowing about God to becoming intimate with God.

The Fire of God

The fire of God does many things in the life of the believer, but there are two key results.

The fire of God ignites our hearts. The apostle Paul urged his young protégé Timothy to stir up the fire in his soul: "I remind you to fan into flame the gift of God, which is in you" (2 Timothy 1:6).

The fire of God exposes our works. "For there is nothing covered that will not be revealed, nor hidden that will not be known" (Luke 12:2, NKJV). "Each one's work will become clear; for the Day will declare it, because it will be revealed by fire; and the fire will test each one's work, of what sort it is" (1 Corinthians 3:13, NKJV).

Seven Ways We Lose Our Spiritual Passion

Since so much of the church today is lacking passion, what are some of the negative habits or practices that cause our passion for God, his work, his presence, and his people to diminish? Sometimes in order to find out more of what we need to do right, we need to consider the things we may be doing wrong. Here are seven passion-losers in your faith experience:

1. **Neglecting the person of God and the practices of faith—God, prayer, and worship.** Overlooking the simplest aspects of faith develops a *shallow* soul.

2. **Centering your life on yourself.** This forms a *shrinking* soul.

3. **Dependence on natural talents and abilities alone.** This leads to a *self-sufficient* soul.

4. **Ethnic exclusivity.** This creates an *isolated* soul.

5. **Overlooking and dishonoring the generations.** This yields an *unsupported* soul.

6. **Disconnecting from community and relationships.** This produces a *selfish* soul.

7. **Conforming to the world, one compromise at a time.** This leads to a *conflicted* soul.

Remember, unless we believe that what is above us is greater than that which is within us, we will succumb to that which is around us.

Glorious Disorder?

The church at Ephesus is a great example of passion lost, a place where one has lost one's "first love" (see Revelation 2:1–7, especially verse 4). It is where we become so comfortable in our faith that things become routine, we engage in vain repetition or in vain practices, and we lose the flavor and the passion of it. And we all must be very careful because we are all susceptible to the deficiencies of the church at Ephesus if we are not intentional every day and self-conscious of that possibility being very real.

It appears that while growing in breadth and width as a church, the Ephesians lost the passionate heights and depths of their faith (see Ephesians 3:18). Jesus called them to renew their passion, to return to their first love, and to rekindle the *Passio Dei*. Charles Spurgeon, often considered the prince of preachers, found that doctrine and sermons alone were not enough. He prayed for his faith to catch fire.

> May God send us a season of glorious disorder! Oh for a sweep of wind that will set the seas in motion and make our ironclad Brethren now lying so quietly at anchor to roll from stem to stern! . . . Oh for fire to fall again—fire which shall affect the most stolid! . . . Oh that such fire might first sit upon the disciples and then fall on all around! . . .
>
> O Spirit of God, You are ready to work with us, today, even as You did then! Delay not, we beseech You, but work at once! Break down every barrier that hinders the incomings of Your might! . . . Give us now both hearts of flame and tongues of fire to preach Your reconciling word for Jesus' sake. Amen.[11]

FEED THE FIRE
Questions to Ignite Growth and Change

1. What do you think the apostle Paul meant when he talked about the depths and the heights of knowing Christ? What were some of the depths and heights that shaped his life?

2. How would you explain the three Os described in this chapter: orthodoxy, orthopraxy, and orthopathy? Which one is the most important? Explain.

3. Which of the seven practices of soul-full faith do you most consistently engage in?

4. Which of the seven practices do you need to focus on more? How so?

5. Do we think enough about the "ferocity" of God? In what ways might our lives and faith be strengthened if we did?

6. What are ways we tend to lose our spiritual passion as Christians?

7. What are some of the best ways to stir our spiritual passion?

4

The Pentecostal Paradox

The greatest growth of all is coming in the Pentecostal or charismatic churches. It is the untold story.
—Rick Warren, in *Time*

They saw what seemed to be tongues of fire that separated and came to rest on each of them.
—Acts 2:3

The freedom of the Holy Spirit and the freeing use of spiritual gifts are key characteristics of rapidly growing Latino faith. In fact, Barna: Hispanics' research found that there are three Cs that describe predominant aspects of Latino faith experience: "Christianity, Catholicism, and charismatic faith."

Barna then notes details. "As for the first 'C,' more than four out of five Hispanics (84%) describe themselves as part of the Christian faith." As to the second C, nearly seven out of ten Hispanics (68 percent) identify with the Roman Catholic Church. The final C represents the Charismatic and Pentecostal groups and practices with which many Hispanics are connected.

The third way of examining the Charismatic movement's influence on Hispanic faith is based on self-identity, what people call themselves. In terms of personal labels, "41% of Christian or Catholic respondents self-identify as charismatic or Pentecostal, saying the terms accurately fit their faith," including "39% of Catholics and 50% of Protestants."[1]

"Uncontrollable Growth"

Today, speaking in tongues and the fostering Pentecostal movement it "evidenced" is sweeping the planet and has been for several decades. Speaking in tongues has carried an iconic and symbolic role in classical Pentecostalism. The movement that began with a handful of tongue-talking worshipers on Azusa Street in Los Angeles in 1906 grew to a following of twelve million by 1972. Today, quite remarkably, Pentecostals in their various forms have reportedly grown to almost 600 million worldwide, approximately one-fourth of all Christendom.

Respected historian Vinson Synan predicts that by the end of the twenty-first century, Pentecostals will encompass half of all Christians in the world. And, although not a member of the Assemblies of God (AG) himself, he also estimates that at her present rate of growth, the AG will become the largest Protestant denomination in the world. Statistics verify this trend.[2]

Today, however, within some Pentecostal groups in America there is a perceived trending away from exercising this gift in public worship; even in self-described "Pentecostal" worship.

Holding Their Tongues?

Speaking in tongues has arguably been the most emphasized charisma of the modern Pentecostal movement. Although the leading Pentecostal denominations in the world all emphasize this gift, some do so more than others. In fact, the largest Pentecostal organization in the world, the AG (Assemblies of God), considers tongues "the initial physical evidence of the baptism in the Holy Spirit," referring to its "distinctive doctrine." It is considered the primary tangible evidence that a Christ-follower has experienced a "second work of grace" called the baptism in the Holy Spirit. This is an experience believers are, according to doctrinal statements, supposed to "ardently expect" and "earnestly seek." Oddly, however, it seems that this hallmark phenomenon over the past couple of decades has arguably on many fronts been deemphasized, displaced, and in some cases, even placed on hold within churches that still consider themselves "Pentecostal."

"The phenomenon [of speaking in tongues] seems much less frequent than a generation or two ago in local churches," said noted Pentecostal theologian Russell Spittler, "especially urban ones or megachurches. Charismatics for the most part do not emphasize the practice nor do they insist on the initial evidence doctrine, which is nevertheless strongly insisted upon within the denominational leadership of the AG. The wide success of denominational and televangelist charismatics, without initial evidence insistence, has isolated mainly North American classical Pentecostal denominations as the lone champions of the doctrine."

Pentecostalism should not be defined by the white Pentecostal church primarily. It seems that the white Pentecostal church in the United States is becoming less and less Pentecostal. It is often "Pentecostal" in name only. The white Pentecostal church is in a state of crisis with much trepidation evident among its leaders. In fact, there is a "don't ask/don't tell" policy mentality about the pneuma. The white Pentecostal church in America has become much more evangelical and non-Spirit-filled. By the end of this century, the white Pentecostal church may be a very small community unless there is a coming back to authentic Pentecostalism.

I (Samuel) see at least three primary reasons for the decreasing dynamic of Pentecostalism in these settings: One, there is a new definition of success. There is this idea that the successful church is all about numbers, and there is a great concern about this. It is the seeker-friendly mind-set on steroids. We say, "God forbid that we permit speaking in tongues." And yet, people are looking for real experiences with God. Unfortunately, many of these leaders believe they can't grow the church with the power of God. Reason two is because of an increasingly sinful culture and moral relativism. Remember, the Spirit is the

Holy Spirit. Churches are trepid over the moving of the Spirit because of the holiness (and I mean authentic biblical holiness) that accompanies it. We don't want to preach on sin. Churches are hesitant to address sin because of the metric of success. It is the consequence of Christian media and competitiveness. American Pentecostalism in recent years has focused more on messaging, branding, and marketing instead of salvation and empowerment. We are in a state of crisis.

Reason three is the sort of generational eclectic framework. There is a definitive chasm between Pentecostal leaders and laypeople as it relates to what people desire to see in Pentecostal worship. Additionally, too often the universities, seminaries, and colleges are not doing a great enough job at revitalizing and affirming Pentecostalism in students. Our schools need to help us prepare next generation Pentecostals.

A Diminishing of the Distinctive?

For Pentecostals, the times have changed. A movement that has experienced rapid growth in the past century in the United States amid periodic controversy and frequent misunderstanding has both influenced existing mainstream church culture and perhaps been influenced by it, as well. Pentecostalism, once quite unaccepted and even spurned by other denominations, has become much more welcomed amid Evangelicals. But has that acceptance come with a price?

Pentecostal and Charismatic expressions of praise and worship have arguably had a great influence on many mainstream churches. Since the Charismatic renewal of the 1970s and the characteristic celebratory forms of worship that accompanied it, worship teams have replaced numerous choirs and organs across the country. From original praise songs borrowed from Christ for the Nations Institute (Texas) in the 1980s, to Hosanna Integrity monthly praise albums of the 1990s, to Hillsong Music and the Passion Movement in the last decade, worship forms have changed significantly. Praises and singing accompanied by upraised hands and clapping have become common fare in many mainline churches that previously were given to more reverential and contemplative forms.

But while more mainstream Evangelical churches have borrowed Charismatic styles of worship and thus become more "pentecostalized," Pentecostal churches also seem to have changed as well, at least in North America. Many report a moving away in public worship gatherings from the more demonstrative expressions of spiritual gifts, such as messages in tongues with interpretation, prayers for healing, and prophecy. In many cases, churches and megachurches have chosen to relegate glossolalia and other charisms to Sunday night services or small groups and, in some cases and settings, according to church historian Dr. Stanley Burgess, "it has virtually disappeared."

Current Assemblies of God national leader, George Wood, explains that the exercise of tongues has been "more limited. There's been a cultural shift in the last thirty years. Sunday morning services used to be for believers, and Sunday night services were more evangelistic. Sunday night services have declined, and now the morning service is more for people to bring friends."[3]

"A Grievous Issue"

Jack Hayford, renowned Pentecostal leader and former president of the Foursquare Church, believes that Pentecostals of all brands in the United States need to reemphasize the work of the Holy Spirit in the life of the believer. He asks, "Why is the church exploding in growth south of the equator in Charismatic and Pentecostal movements? It is because those people go after the whole package and live in it. There is a sense of quest. There is no sense of a need to appease social tastes or acceptability. Our tendency towards such concerns in the United States is a grievous issue to me."

Traditionally the hallmark distinctive of Pentecostal and Charismatic churches has been a personal experience in the Holy Spirit evidenced by super-natural expressions and gifts. So, what might the reasons be among some Pentecostals for pulling away or shifting their characteristic practices of speaking in tongues?

Among the possible factors contributing to this change in the practice of speaking in tongues may be the following.

The Evangelicalization of Pentecostalism

"From WWII to Vietnam, the evangelicalization of Pentecostalism occurred," said Spittler. "Then, from Vietnam till now, we've seen the pentecostalization of evangelicalism. Each movement [has] influenced the other."

Spittler's theory seems to hold true here. Pentecostals, once eschewed for their unusual expressions of worship, have become much more mainstream and sophisticated in recent years. One observer notes that Pentecostals used to feel like the "weird uncle" of the Evangelical family; now, in some ways, they just might have become the favorite son.

Donald E. Miller, USC professor and researcher of Pentecostal trends, recently stated, "In the U.S., the historical Pentecostal denominations have tended to routinize. They tend to look much more like mainline Protestant churches and the rapid growth rates tend to level off. Which is true with the Assemblies of God."[4]

Seeker-Friendliness

Understandably, pastoral leaders have looked to "successful models of church growth" and often borrowed heavily. Among them have been Jack Hyle's bus-outreach model, Bill Hybel's seeker-friendly model, and Rick Warren's purpose-driven model. Sometimes, however, the incorporation of new models of ministry, and especially comprehensive ones, have become dominant forces of change to the diminishing of prior "Pentecostal distinctives." While adding some things, others may have been lost.

"The search for acceptability and success has impacted the passion that sparks the gospel," says Hayford. "Seeker-friendly focuses became a substitute for [Pentecostals] who had lost the baby in the bathwater of their own tradition. They adopted a framework of ministry that diminished discipleship and, along with it, the sense of need for the Baptism in the Holy Spirit."

A New Technology and Media Focus

Our media-saturated and video-driven culture has provided a wealth of tools that have been incorporated into church worship services. Staff, resources, and countless hours are now poured into tedious preparations for not only worship but worship productions that are finely edited, patiently rehearsed, and powerfully projected. Services, sermons, and songs are now often expected to "pop" and excite the audience's supposed insatiable thirst for eye, and ear, candy. In some cases the sensational may have displaced the supernatural. Isaiah warned against man's efforts to conjure "fire" on his own instead of waiting for the fire that God's Spirit alone can bring:

> Who among you fears the LORD
> and obeys the word of his servant?
> Let him who walks in the dark,
> who has no light,
> trust in the name of the LORD
> and rely on his God.
> But now, all you who light fires
> and provide yourselves with flaming torches,
> go, walk in the light of your fires
> and of the torches you have set ablaze.
> This is what you shall receive from my hand:
> You will lie down in torment.
> (Isaiah 50:10–11)

Samuel Chadwick saw this coming many decades ago and described it not as "strange fire" but rather as "stage" fire:

Earth-kindled fires burn fiercely, but they burn out. They allure to deeper darkness. Lights that glare and dazzle blind the eyes. Artificial excitement destroys spiritual sensibility. Satiated desire fails. When religion turns to humanity for its inspiration and to the world for its power, God is dethroned and the sanctuary becomes a secularized fellowship. . . .

Stage fire is a trick. In the absence of the supernatural, earnest souls may turn to the best substitutes they can find, and believe they are doing God's service. When the fires of spiritual devotion go out, ritualism finds its opportunity. Aids to voluptuous meditation take the place of reverent adoration. If there be no power to cast out devils, transform sinners and save souls, there are other ministries within reach. John did no miracle; may not a ministry of "water baptism" avail for our day and generation? If we have no fire from on high by which men's souls can be saved, there are minds to be instructed and bodies to be fed. Churches destitute of divine fire may devote themselves fervently to good works, but stage fire is a mockery and a pretense. Stage-lights have found their way into the Church. The red glare dazzles, but it does not burn. Fireworks are brilliant, but they end with the hour. No ideals are kindled, no ministry impelled, no sacrifice inspired. The pretense of spirituality is the worst profanity. Strange fire is less offensive than stage fire. A religion of mere emotion and sensationalism is the most terrible of all curses that can come upon any people. The absence of reality is sad enough, but the aggravation of pretense is a deadly sin.[5]

Undertaught/Underchallenged

A 2008 survey on the state of discipleship, commissioned by the AG Discipleship Ministries Agency and conducted by Ed Stetzer of LifeWay Christian

Resources, revealed that while 90 percent of AG pastors claim to teach regularly on the subject of the baptism of the Holy Spirit, only 28 percent strongly agreed that they regularly take time to pray for people to receive the Holy Spirit. And only about half of those who attend worship services claim to have been baptized in the Holy Spirit.[6]

Billy Wilson, president of Oral Roberts University and Empowered21, conducted a broad set of focus groups on Pentecostal college and university campuses a few years ago. Among the trends the research revealed was "a decline in teaching and preaching on the Holy Spirit from the pulpit." Wilson says, "This generation is highly interested in the supernatural and the Holy Spirit, but are unfortunately more ignorant of such things. They say, 'I want it but just don't know much about it.'"

Control

There are aspects of the person and ministry of the Holy Spirit within faith gatherings that call for an openness to spontaneity and a relinquishment of some of the tightly gripped controls on culture. While the Spirit of God is clearly an organized and sovereign collaborative amid the members of the Trinity, there are seasons of "suddenlys" that often characterize His ministry and movements. This occurs from "a violent wind" (Acts 2:2) on the Day of Pentecost to the unexpected soul stirrings of Cornelius's household (see Acts 10–11) evidenced by tongues. God's Spirit is free to move.

Before I (Robert) experienced an infilling of the Spirit, church for me was always the place I went simply *to hear what the preacher would say next*; now it was the place I went to hear a soul-stirring sermon, yes, but also to *see what the Spirit would do next*. Have we lost some of this?

Concern over Excess

The open worship environments associated with Pentecostalism have fostered spontaneous expressions of faith, but have sometimes spawned excesses. Spittler acknowledges, however, "The AG establishment has saved much of

Pentecostalism from weird forms of [excess and] supernaturalism—extreme forms of dictatorial guidance cloaked as shepherding, too otherworldly forms of 'Latter Rain,' and anti-Trinitarian conceptions of the Godhead, among others."

Warren's Advice to Pentecostals

"You don't need to change any of your Pentecostal practices." So was the advice from a leading Evangelical pastor, Rick Warren, to the gathering of Assemblies of God (AG) pastors in Phoenix, Arizona, at their biennial council. Urging the ministers not to abandon their use of spiritual gifts, he said, "What you *do* need to do [instead] is explain them. Do not compromise what God has called you to do; simply make it explainable."[7]

While reminding AG leaders that healthy churches focus on five purposes (worship, fellowship, discipleship, ministry, and evangelism), Warren suggested that Pentecostal church health also means a sixth focus: "to be Pentecostal." He used the analogy of a person's first visit to the opera to explain the importance of helping newcomers to Pentecostal charismata understand what is going on: "You wouldn't ask the vocalists in an opera to sing in English or to change their tune; you simply want a little help in understanding what's going on and what it means."

While operas are beautiful expressions of the Italian spirit, they can be tough experiences to navigate for the novice. Understanding this art form requires patience and a willingness to learn. With the right assistance, the opera can lead the viewer to greater understanding and self-awareness. Warren offers a clever and considerate analogy to the world of Pentecostalism.

But has today's Pentecostal tune changed? And just what has warranted such words from Warren?

For Pentecostals, the times have changed. A movement that has experienced rapid growth in the past century in the United States amid periodic controversy and frequent misunderstanding has both influenced existing mainstream church culture and perhaps been influenced by it as well. Pentecostalism, once quite unaccepted and even spurned by other denominations, has become much more welcomed amid Evangelicals than ever before. But, we ask again, has that acceptance come with a price?

As to how a Pentecostal church can see the operation of spiritual gifts revitalized without scaring off or confusing new visitors in worship services, Warren simply suggests providing some clarification and explanation of "the opera." Several churches list a handful of FAQs in their bulletins.

And, as for an explanation for dynamic gifts such as speaking in tongues, the apostle Paul gave advice to the charismata-consumed Corinthian church somewhat similar to Warren's: "If anyone speaks in a tongue . . . someone must interpret. If there is no interpreter, the speaker should keep quiet in the church and speak to himself and God" (1 Corinthians 14:27–28).

Perhaps most surprising of all Warren's admonitions at the council was this one: *"Don't lose your Pentecostal distinctive."* Could it be that God has brought a fresh word to Pentecostals in North America and that he has chosen to use an unexpected source? While Elijah sought for a sign from God, he looked for it in the "wind," the "earthquake," and the "fire." It came, instead, in an unexpected "still, small voice." It may be that in this instance God didn't send a message in tongues or a prophetic word to challenge North American Pentecostals, but rather a clear message from the plainspoken tongue of a Southern Baptist pastor.

Uncontrollable

In his book *Spirit-Empowered Christianity in the 21st Century,* Vinson Synan notes that "the greatest growth [among Pentecostals and Charismatics] has been and continues to be in Africa, Asia, and Latin America." He adds, "The growth has been much smaller in North America and Europe."[8] One comparison, for instance, is that more people now attend Assemblies of God (AG) churches in one Latin American city than in the entire United States! The AG has just under three million adherents in the United States, while São Paulo, Brazil, holds weekly services for more than three million. Brazil, "by conservative estimates, has over 20 million adherents. In fact, over 95 percent of people affiliated with the Assemblies of God worldwide are now located outside the United States."[9]

Just what accounts for the dramatic differences in rates of growth among Pentecostals in the United States and overseas? Synan states that "it seems that signs and wonders are more prevalent in less developed parts of the world." The supernatural in general is more acknowledged in many spheres of life and faith in the "developing" parts of the world.

David Barrett's *World Christian Encyclopedia* confirms that the widest growth in evangelism regularly correlates with the welcoming of the Holy Spirit's ministry of the supernatural—through gifts, signs, and wonders. He further states that "many situations of uncontrollable growth" are occurring where the Holy Spirit's gifts are allowed.

Doctrine and Experience

Harvard professor and life-long observer of Pentecostalism Harvey Cox noted that for many years in the Pentecostal movement, experience came before doctrine. In other words, people experienced the life-changing power of the Holy Spirit in their lives and then asked, "What meaneth this?" (Acts 2:12, KJV). This led to a search for biblical truth and the proper foundation for the experience. Today, however, Cox observes that many so-called Pentecostals are trying to put doctrine before experience. He questions how helpful this is for the movement.[10]

A. W. Tozer warned against the dangers of theology devoid of passionate intimacy with God:

God will not hold us responsible to understand the mysteries of election, predestination, and the divine sovereignty. The best and safest way to deal with these truths is to raise our eyes to God and in deepest reverence say, *O LORD, thou knowest.* Those things belong to the deep and mysterious profoundness of God's omniscience. Prying into them may make theologians, but it will rarely make saints.[11]

We believe Millennials in North America are primed for a Pentecostal experience. In fact, our observations in churches and Christian university settings worldwide reveal that youth today are much more passionate in their worship than their parents' generation. However, they are also more independent in their approaches to faith and less willing to fit into anyone's mold. They are ready and hungry for the *Passio Dei*!

Hayford sees tongues as the most identifiable phenomenological distinctive among Pentecostals. "Without initial physical evidence [that is, tongues], then there would be no distinctive Pentecostal or Charismatic renewal today. The pivotal point is this: Discipleship doesn't happen without Spirit fullness. I see 'Pentecostal', however, as more of a verb than a noun. And, I believe the new generation is ready to go there."

"Our generation is probably more like our grandparents' than our parents'," said Chad Lashley, a twenty-something pastoral ministries student at Southeastern University who was raised in an Assemblies of God church. "We really want to see an authentic work of God in our lives. We are tired of 'a good worship service' being determined by chill bumps. If there is one thing that is true about our generation it is that we don't mind being different. You'll notice most of us have a style of our own. We're not afraid of being Pentecostal."

FEED THE FIRE
Questions to Ignite Growth and Change

1. What are the three Cs of Latino faith experience as described by Barna: Hispanics? To which of these do you most relate?
2. How would you describe Pentecostalism and the role it plays in today's church?
3. What advice does Rick Warren give to Pentecostals today?
4. Is there a diminishing of Pentecostal practices among some Pentecostal or Charismatic groups today? If so, what are the reasons for this?
5. Why is Pentecostalism so appealing to Latino Christians? Why do you think it is exploding in growth globally?
6. What could American Pentecostals learn from those in Latin America?
7. Has media production and "stage fires" taken the place of the work of the Holy Spirit in our worship services today? What needs to change to open ourselves and our worship gatherings to more of the fullness of God's Spirit?

PART TWO

Uniting with Passion

Loving Your Neighbor as Yourself

The Cries of a Community

I have indeed seen the misery of my people. . . . I have
heard them crying out . . . and I am concerned about
their suffering.

—Exodus 3:7

When Juana Bordas was a seven-year-old girl, her family moved to a new part of town and she entered a new school. Although the distance in miles to the new location was not far, the cultural difference was like crossing an ocean. The first day Juana "walked into second grade to see a whole sea of white faces." Desperate to "be accepted and to succeed in school," Juana "stopped speaking Spanish, learned to act like the other kids, and even became embarrassed by [her] immigrant family."[1]

There are so many other little girls and boys, as well as grown men and women, who carry much pain and struggle within their hearts as they try to adapt and adjust, to find a welcome and a home in a new land, in a new place. Don't you wonder just how many millions of those internal hurts, worries, and cries go unnoticed and unheard? How many of them wake up each morning and go to bed each night carrying an extra emotional load while feeling so much like a strange person in a strange land, just wanting so much to feel at home? The Old Testament tells of a time when God's people, the Hebrews, found themselves facing an interesting set of circumstances in a strange land, a land that at first was a land of provision during a time of need. Through Joseph and his emergence in Egypt as a key leader, his father and family found a land of refuge and provision during a great famine. When they arrived in Egypt, the strange land was a place of promise and provision. However, over the coming years it would become a place of their enslavement as they came to know it not as the land of provision but the land of bondage.

The cries of the Hebrew nation rose to a boiling point and caught the attention of God. In fact, it so arrested his attention that he appointed a deliverer, Moses, to go and help rescue them. Here's the way the Bible describes God's response to their cries:

> The LORD said, "*I have indeed seen the misery of my people* in Egypt. *I have heard them crying out* because of their slave drivers, and *I am concerned about their suffering.* So I have come down to rescue them from the hand of the Egyptians and to bring them up out of that land into a good and spacious land, a land flowing with milk and honey— the home of the Canaanites, Hittites, Amorites, Perizzites, Hivites and Jebusites. And now the cry of the Israelites has reached me, and I have seen the way the Egyptians are oppressing them. So now, go. I am sending you to Pharaoh to bring my people the Israelites out of Egypt." (Exodus 3:7–10)

God Hears

"I have heard them crying out . . ." Thousands of years ago, God could hear the silent, and not so silent, cries of his children as they were weighed down under oppression. He heard it and was "concerned about their suffering" (verse 7). So concerned was he that he "[came] down to rescue them from the hand of the Egyptians to bring them up out of that land into a good and spacious land, a land flowing with milk and honey." He said, "Now the cry of the Israelites has reached me, and I have seen the way the Egyptians are oppressing them. So now, go. I am sending you to Pharaoh to bring my people the Israelites out of

Egypt" (verses 9–10). God heard the cries of his people and then responded. He is doing the same thing today.

Consider a few important details in this story:

- God heard his people crying under the oppression of a foreign land.
- God was concerned for those who were hurting and crying.
- This passage in Exodus does *not* say that he was concerned about the political system or the rules and policies and laws of Egypt. No, he was concerned for his people.
- God was so concerned that he *came down* in order to *bring them up*.

God hears the cries of Latinos and Hispanics today. He knows the challenges and difficult feelings of displacement.

The depths of passion for God stirring today in the Latino church are not the only soulful sounds being heard. There are other "cries" coming from the hearts of Latinos and Latino communities all over the world. While sweeping revival is occurring throughout the Latino world today, there are also desperate struggles taking place: social struggles, financial struggles, political struggles, family struggles, and more. While God is pouring his grace out, so many despots, drug lords, and demons are still determined to use and abuse people God created to be his image-bearers.

A Certain Cry

Bianca Juarez Olthoff recalls that when she was a child her father could recognize each of his five children's unique cries all the way from their rooms. When any of them were afraid or needed him, he knew just who it was from the sound of the cries. To this day his children still call him for advice, direction, and emotional support. Olthoff also notes that

the Bible makes a clear distinction between *prayer* and *crying out*.
The children of Israel cried out to be free from bondage and the Lord

rescued them (Ex. 3:7). David cried out for healing and God spared his life (Ps. 30:2).

[David] used [the Hebrew word] *qara* frequently, and I believe it was because he knew crying out came before worship. "*Call* upon Me in the day of trouble," he wrote in Psalm 50:15, "I will deliver you, and you shall glorify Me" (NKJV, emphasis mine). David penned this in Psalm 145:18: "The LORD is near to all those who *call* upon Him, to all who *call* upon Him in truth" (NKJV, emphasis mine).[2]

If you could plug an earphone into the hearts of Latinos in America and across the world today, you would hear many cries. There are burdens, worries, and concerns that many feel but few are willing to express. As concerned followers of Christ, let's consider what some of those cries may be and how we may respond.

Latino Cry 1: Disregarded and Dishonored

One of the major cries coming from the hearts of many Latino immigrants living in the United States is a cry of *loneliness*. Martha Lesperance-Garcia, a missionary who coordinates church plants among ethnic minorities in the Gulf region of Alabama, lives in a city with immigrants from sixty-two nations—almost none of which are represented in local churches. She notes that fewer than one in ten immigrants there will ever have an American friend. Christians who serve a God who "sets the lonely in families [Psalm 68:6] must see the immigrant and be willing to reach out," Garcia says.[3] It is safe to say the church simply isn't reaching them. This is the same church which Jesus directed to "love your neighbor as yourself" (Matthew 22:39; Mark 12:31).

"About half of Hispanics in the US (52%) say they have experienced discrimination or have been treated unfairly because of their race or ethnicity." About 58 percent of both Hispanics and blacks "say race relations in the U.S. are generally bad." Most Hispanics in the survey say that the best way to deal with race relations is for people to "focus on what different racial and ethnic groups have in common."[4]

Juana Goes to Her First Social Event

"As a child, I could total up my 'social disabilities,'" Juana Bordas says. "I was poor, Brown, small boned, short, and a girl. My mother spoke broken English. I didn't think I was very smart." Many years after this experience, Juana today recognizes that she experienced a "cultural inferiority complex."

As a young teenager, dealing with the awkwardness of that season of life and more, Juana was invited by a "well-to-do Anglo cheerleader" at her school to attend a party. She was excited about the opportunity, and her mother took her to a department store to buy a dress especially for it. Such a purchase was a privilege she had never imagined, and she had no idea how her mom could afford it. But once she chose a "red cotton dress with black and brown stripes and a little brown bowtie on the collar," she was so happy that she and her mother "danced around the store." The moment was a fiesta all its own.

However, Juana was mortified the night she walked into the party and found a room full of "rich girls dressed in fancy taffeta and silk." She was so embarrassed that she "hid in a bathroom all night [and refused] to come out." In similar situations, minority children often think the same things as Juana did: "'I am not good enough,' 'Something is wrong with me,' 'They are better than me,' or 'I won't amount to much.'"[5]

Latino Cry 2: Losing Their Youth

There is also a great concern among Latinos today that they are losing their youth, losing the next generation who are leaving the faith. Many Latinos are ever so concerned their children are lost in unbelief, moral relativism, cultural decadence, spiritual apathy, ecclesiastical lukewarmness, sexual immorality, drug abuse, violent behavior, and the lack of a commitment to education, home, family, and faith. These are some of the cries coming out of the Latino community in the United States and around the world.

Barna: Hispanics research noted a falling off from the church by some Hispanic Americans. It also showed that many unchurched Latinos hold negative or "lukewarm" views toward Christianity and churches in general. A disillusionment with faith is "even more pronounced among Catholics."[6]

> Relative to the national norm, a high proportion of Hispanics say they
> have dropped out of the church at some point in their lives. Even of
> those who continue attending church, just one out of three Hispanics
> would be considered practicing Christians. Unchurched Hispanics
> seem to have a less positive view of the Christian church than un-
> churched U.S. adults. Just 17% of Hispanics have a very favorable
> view of the Christian church.[7]

Among those Hispanics in America who have experienced a "religious switching" or change, "the biggest gains have been among the unaffiliated (a net gain of 17 percentage points) and Protestants (a net gain of seven points). Catholics, by contrast, have had a net loss of 25 percentage points among the native born." Perhaps even more interesting in this Pew study[8] were the reasons those Hispanics who have switched their religious status cited for doing so. Of six possible reasons offered on the survey:

> 55% say they just gradually "drifted away" from the religion in which
> they were raised, and 52% say they stopped believing in the teachings
> of their childhood religion.
>
> In addition, nearly a third (31%) say they found a congregation
> that reaches out and helps members more, while roughly a fifth say
> the decision was associated with a "deep personal crisis" (23%) or with
> moving to a new community (19%). About one-in-ten (9%) say that
> marrying someone who practices a different faith was an important
> reason for leaving their childhood religion. . . .

Latinos who have left the Catholic Church are especially likely to say that an important reason was that they stopped believing in its teachings; 63% of former Catholics who are now unaffiliated and 57% of former Catholics who are now Protestants give this reason for having left the church.

In addition, 49% of Hispanics who were raised as Catholics and have become Protestants say that an important factor was finding a church that "reaches out and helps its members more."

In this same survey, "three-quarters of Latino adults . . . (77%) say they were raised as Catholics, while just over half (55%) currently describe themselves as Catholics. Roughly a quarter of Latinos were raised Catholic and have left the faith (24%), while just 2% were raised in some other faith and have converted to Catholicism, for a net decline of 22 percentage points."

The concern Hispanics have over losing their children to faithlessness or to the spirit of the age (see 2 Corinthians 4:4) extends beyond Millennials and to other groups. Barna: Hispanics reports that "many unchurched Latinos express lukewarm or negative views toward Christianity and toward Christian churches in general."[9] However, a disillusionment with church and faith is even more pronounced among Catholics.

A Barna: Hispanics study confirms a falling off from the church by some Hispanic Americans. It affirms that compared to "the national norm of 59% among all U.S. adults," "two out of every three Hispanics (67%) say they have gone through a period of life when they dropped out of attending church, after having gone regularly."[10]

Latino Cry 3: Immigration Issues

Living in a nation of immigrants, it is ironic how little we Americans sometimes know or understand about immigration and how it has occurred. For example, Jesse Miranda, an elder statesman in the Hispanic church in America, did not come from Latin America; he was more accurately acculturated here because

> the first Hispanics to become part of this country did not do so by migration but were rather engulfed by the United States in its process of expansion—sometimes by purchase, sometimes by military conquest, and sometimes by simple annexation of territories no one was strong enough to defend. Even without turning back to history, this is clear when one looks at a map of the United States and finds in it such names as Florida, California, Nevada, Colorado, Los Angeles, San Francisco, San Diego, [and] Sacramento.[11]

Ultimately the United States by various means "came to possess vast lands inhabited by people of Hispanic culture. Thus in the beginning it was not Hispanics who migrated to this nation, but this nation that migrated to Hispanic lands."[12] Or, as Miranda, born in Mexico, puts it, "When I became an American, I did not cross the border, but the border crossed me."[13]

Miranda, a key leader in the Hispanic church in America, has led multiple initiatives in education that have resulted in centers in universities and colleges devoted to welcoming and developing Hispanic students. However, he notes that one of the most difficult cultural aspects for Latinos in America is that they are not always greeted with the warmest welcome. He says,

> Anglos often live very private lives. They tend to live in little circles. But we live in a *barrio* and have to connect and exchange in those settings. Churches don't seem to have a history of bridges.[14]

Immigrants in America suffered under the labor of *perpetual limbo* because of the lack of immigration reform in the US Congress. Immigrants today in America suffer from two things. First, those who are illegal would like to be documented, especially those who have been here for years and whose children were raised here. They were basically given a "wink-wink/nod-nod" to "come on in" and work for us in our service industry (restaurants, farms, fields, and so on) twenty or twenty-five years ago, and now they are being asked to be deported. They would like to do things right and become legal and pay fines, or maybe go back to their country for one day, if it guarantees they could come back and work toward becoming a resident and maybe a citizen twenty years down the road. That's the reality.

Second, there are the immigrants who have come here legally but are also marginalized because they are immigrants. Now with the election of Donald Trump and the verbiage and rhetoric regarding Latinos and immigrants, it is a difficult season indeed. It is arguably the most difficult season for immigrants to be in America for the past hundred years.

What we often miss within this issue of immigration, however, is the fact that the majority of Latino immigrants in America are God-fearing, hardworking, family-loving individuals. The vast majority (over 95 percent) have come into America not for the purpose of doing anything egregious, but just for survivability and to give their kids a future. They have no intention whatsoever of changing the political landscape of America or of assuring that the Democrats will have power for thirty years to come. All they want to do is provide food for their children, provide clothes for their children, and see their children do better and go further than they have. And they come from very precarious and dangerous places in the world and want their children to survive. This is not even about thriving right now; it is about their children surviving and living long and healthy, vibrant lives. That's the other side of the story.

Our Response to Immigrants

To consider the issue as immigration alone is to depersonalize or dehumanize it. The real issue and the real need each of us must face is not immigration but the immigrant or immigrants, the people who find themselves displaced and struggling to find a home.

According to Barna Research, 97 percent of Hispanic immigrants say they are proud of their heritage. Additionally, more of them identify first as Hispanic or Latino (54 percent) than as Christian or Catholic (24 percent) or even American (20 percent).[15]

But how should we, as Christians, respond to the cries of immigrants? From Leviticus 19 to Matthew 25 to Romans 13, the Scriptures are full of challenging words and directives we need to hear and respond to.

> When a stranger sojourns with you in your land, you shall not do him wrong. You shall treat the stranger who sojourns with you as the native among you, and you shall love him as yourself, for you were strangers in the land of Egypt: I am the LORD your God. (Leviticus 19:33–34, ESV)

> Then the King will say to those on his right, "Come, you who are blessed by my Father, inherit the kingdom prepared for you from the foundation of the world. For I was hungry and you gave me food, I was thirsty and you gave me drink, I was a stranger and you welcomed me." (Matthew 25:34-35, ESV)

> Let every person be subject to the governing authorities. For there is no authority except from God, and those that exist have been instituted by God. Therefore whoever resists the authorities resists what God has appointed, and those who resist will incur judgment. For rulers are not a terror to good conduct, but to bad. Would you have no fear of the one who is in authority? Then do what is good, and you will receive his approval, for he is God's servant for your good. (Romans 13:1–4, ESV)

Despite some popularized notions to the opposite, most Hispanics possess a fairly balanced view toward immigration. Barna Research found that most Hispanics' underlying wishes and views toward immigration reform reflect balancing ideals that consider both sides of the argument. Two-thirds (65 percent) see that they have a biblical responsibility to be hospitable to immigrants and strangers. Yet, more than half (55 percent) understand and believe that there is "a biblical responsibility to follow the laws and rules of the government."[16] So, how can Christians and church leaders today respond to the cries of immigrants in our country?

A Kingdom Culture, a Kingdom Response

Eventually, in the wilderness wanderings, God called on Moses to develop a kingdom culture among the Hebrew children. It was to be a community and culture centered around *the presence of God,* represented by the ark of the covenant that sat within the holy of holies. This leadership model taught Moses about the power of a covenant with God in the life of a leader. Amid the Hebrew ethos, Moses saw God *promising a covenant* of love to his people. It was not without its challenges.

Although America is a nation made up of immigrants, the term *immigrant* has in many places today become a term of derision. Not many years ago, many Christians and church leaders in the United States were celebrating the fact that through immigration, the nations were coming to America. Neil Diamond made famous the phrase "They're Coming to America" as a theme song for celebrating the faith-inspired journey of immigrants. Even the Statue of Liberty is a symbol of welcome so strong that emblazoned on its pedestal is the famed inscription:

> Give me your tired, your poor,
> Your huddled masses yearning to breathe free,
> The wretched refuse of your teeming shore.
> Send these, the homeless, tempest-tost to me,
> I lift my lamp beside the golden door![17]

A Torch or a Shield?

The new realities of a world reeling from terrorism and political disunity have many questioning just how wise it is to be so welcoming. For many, the Statue of Liberty holding a torch to the sky to light the way for the "huddled masses yearning to breathe free" and welcoming "the wretched refuse" of the "teeming shore" of other nations may not strike the same patriotic chord it once did in the hearts of many. Some, perhaps, would think it wiser for Lady Liberty to carry a shield instead of a torch.

Thought leader and founder of Q Ideas, Gabe Lyons, warns that we always need to be suspect of fear:

> We know that fear comes from the enemy. So, we have to check ourselves to ask where this fear is coming from. Is it a false-placed confidence that I am the one who "protects" my family? We should never sacrifice the opportunity to express God's love out of fear that something possibly should happen down the road. This is the risk every missionary takes and those who choose to love. Love is a risk.[18]

Ultimately, the most important "policies" are not the ones that our government establishes nationally but the ones that every Christian establishes by personal practice. In other words, a new protective law alone set up by government may guard our borders, but it will not save souls. To do that, every Christian must choose to love, care, and be genuinely concerned about the cries of the people around them. We must hear the cries of those who struggle and suffer. We must choose to carry a torch of passion called *love* and serve the pressing needs of our neighbors every day in every way we can.

FEED THE FIRE
Questions to Ignite Growth and Change

1. If you could hear today in your community the soul cries God hears, what would they sound like? What are people desperate for?

2. What are some of the soul cries of Latinos today? How can churches and Christians respond to these needs?

3. Are Latinos disregarded and dishonored in America today? How so?

4. What must it be like to be an alien in a foreign land? Have you ever felt this way?

5. How would God have us respond to immigrants, to foreigners in our midst?

6. How do we "love our neighbor as ourselves" and protect our children at the same time?

7. What are ways in which we are losing our youth today? To what are we losing them? How can we respond to this need?

Introducing Billy Graham to MLK

Had it not been for the ministry of my good friend Dr. Billy Graham, my work in the Civil Rights Movement would not have been as successful as it has been.
—Martin Luther King Jr.

Christianity is not a white man's religion. . . . Christ belongs to all people; He belongs to the whole world.
—Billy Graham

What America needs is a generation committed to marrying the evangelistic message of Billy Graham with the prophetic activism of Dr. King.
—Samuel Rodriguez

Eleven o'clock Sunday morning is the most segregated hour in America,' declared civil-rights leader Martin Luther King Jr. in a well-known line he used a number of times. What is not so well know is that the remark was first made by someone else in a 1950s *Reader's Digest* article on racism. The article was written by King's friend, evangelist Billy Graham."[1]

In a sense, Graham and King became partners in ministry, though most people never recognized this. Our more familiar views are of Graham as a gospel evangelist and of King as a social activist, yet both served with astounding impact as Christian ministers with concern for racial reconciliation. While white Christians in years past identified more with Graham and black Christians more with King, in many cases, we find that Latino Evangelicals today desire a hybrid form of Christianity: a King-Graham ethic and practice, which blend help and hope, grace and truth, righteousness and justice. Graham and King were two men contrasted in their methods but complementary in their goals in so many ways.

The Pen and the Sword

"The pen is mightier than the sword"—so wrote the novelist and playwright Edward Bulwer-Lytton in 1839. Those words were never truer than when Thomas Paine wrote his classic little book entitled *Common Sense*. At that time this treatise on a rationale for freedom from British monarchial tyrannies became the best-selling nonfiction book in US history. It is said that upon its release, you could find people standing on tree stumps and tables reading it out loud to groups throughout towns and cities alike. Pastors read it to their congregations from their pulpits.

The year *before* it was written, there was very little serious thought of declaring independence or forming a separate nation. The year *after,* however, 1776, it was on almost everyone's mind. John Adams summed it up well when he said, "Without the pen of the author of 'Common Sense,' the sword of Washington would have been raised in vain."[2]

It could be said that the will of an emerging nation was nurtured and readied by the principles of Paine. Once the will was certain and steeled, the nation was then ready to march. The minds had to be convinced in order for the hearts and hands to be able to engage the challenges and opportunities of the moment.

So, the pen of Paine and the sword of Washington. The preaching of Graham and the stand of King: both with different gifts but very similar and complementary missions.

Historically, white Evangelicals built a public identity around a two-theme platform agenda—the sanctity of life and traditional marriage. On the other side of the aisle, progressive Evangelicals and black Protestants coalesced around socioeconomic issues such as health care, education, and poverty alleviation. Brown Christians, particularly Hispanic Evangelicals, are poised to redraw the moral map with a commitment to reconcile both sides, working within a framework of both righteousness and justice.

Millennials are uniquely positioned to combine a Graham-King strategy of gospel ministry in their communities. In fact, I (Sam) am often asked, "What is a Hispanic born-again Christian? How will you define your community?" The answer lies embedded in a simple recipe: a Hispanic Christian is what you get when you take Billy Graham and Martin Luther King Jr., put them in a blender, and place salsa on top! It may sound funny to you, but it is true.

The Latino Hybrid

On cultural issues, the Graham-King hybrid generation stands unequivocally as a vigorous pro-life movement that extends from womb to tomb. This new pro-life movement does not regard health care, education, and poverty alleviation as secondary issues to sanctity of life and marriage but rather as top-tier extensions of a truly pro-life platform.

With respect to marriage, the hybrid generation defends traditional marriage while simultaneously repudiating homophobia and supporting legislation that protects all citizens from discrimination in the workplace, regardless of sexual orientation, and secures the civil rights of all Americans. As a result, both political parties will be pressed to gravitate toward a centrist platform in order to engage this emerging generation of Evangelical voters.

"Hispanics will bring their cultural values to bear on Evangelical Christianity with the influence of their collective worldview," said Albert Reyes, president of Buckner Children and Family Services. "Latino Evangelical Christians will be more interested in the welfare of the community at large than their own personal welfare. Hispanics will help Evangelical congregations gravitate toward a balanced application of the gospel to include issues of social justice and equality for everyone in the community. Social issues will take center stage in congregations because the Scripture bears witness to Jesus' focus on the poor, the prisoner, the blind, and the oppressed."

Marrying the Messages

We believe the Millennial generation and the one following them, the Homelanders (that is, Gen Z), are ready to marry the evangelistic message of Billy Graham with the prophetic activism of Dr. King. This is true of emerging Latino Americans and of emerging generations in general. Now is the time to reconcile the message with the march, the way with the dream, the call for salvation with the call for justice, the activism and the altar, and the song of redemption with the song of deliverance. By loving our neighbors, by mending those abandoned on the road to Jericho, this next generation will sing both "There Is Room at the Cross" and "We Shall Overcome."

We are convinced the next great movement in America will not be a reformed Democratic Party nor a revitalized Republican Party, but rather a Christ-centered, Bible-based, Spirit-empowered movement committed to righteousness and justice in the name of Jesus! The most important platform will not stem from the agenda of the donkey or the elephant, but will be the agenda of the Lamb.[3] The desire for such is present within the hearts of emerging generations. It is palpable. It is time to see the psalmist's vision made real: "Righteousness and justice are the foundation of your throne. Unfailing love and truth walk before you as attendants" (Psalm 89:14, NLT).

Modern Evangelicalism in America has been a great and contemporary tool in God's hands for the saving of souls. From the theology of Jonathan Edwards to the preaching of Charles Finney, Billy Sunday, and Billy Graham, millions have heard and responded to the gospel with belief and trust in Jesus.

However, during this same time many Evangelicals, while underlining the importance of the sinner's prayer and repentance, at times held the need for compassion in their communities somewhat at bay. Instead of hearing the cries of the hurting and lonely, too often the church relegated such responses to the government or to social programs. While government by way of taxation does carry the ability to distribute financial aid and sustenance, it is not equipped to provide what the heart most desperately needs: *hope*.

With the founding of social entitlements such as welfare and Social Security in the 1930s, in some ways, whether intentionally or inadvertently, it was easier for the church to assign the gospel and the work of the church to purely eternal or salvific purposes. We would preach to *save souls* and leave it to the government to come up with the programs and funding to *save lives*. This in many ways brought a division to the considerations and the applications of the gospel in life, faith, and culture. It was as if we missed the message of the Lord's Prayer, and instead, by our lack of action, we prayed,

Let your kingdom . . . stay right where it is;
Let your will . . . just be done in heaven and not down here.

While the importance of conversion was underlined, all too often the vital right-now aspects of care, community, and compassion were overlooked. The sinner's prayer and altar calls were more desirable than the pressing sustenance needs of widows, orphans, and the poor. Perhaps starting churches in more up-and-coming demographic areas and preaching to the well-to-do was more intriguing than bringing "good news to the poor . . . [binding] up the broken-hearted . . . [proclaiming] liberty to the captives, and the opening of the prison to those who are bound" (Isaiah 61:1, ESV).

In too many cases, the white church just wanted to give people "hope" and the black church just wanted to give them "help." Today, Latinos are instead underlining the need to do both while calling it the *Kingdom of God*.

A Generational Awakening

"There is a huge awakening for social concern today," says noted Pentecostal leader Jack Hayford, "especially from age 30 and down. It is profoundly present and it is a welcomed renewal."[4] But this isn't the first time such a groundswell of compassionate ministry has marked Pentecostalism. Hayford, a leader in the Foursquare Church, recalls the hugely successful "commissary ministry" of Pentecostal revivalist Aimee Semple McPherson: "It touched millions during the [Great] Depression. It has significantly marked our movement. It spread over the first half of the Twentieth Century." McPherson's compassionate work was carried out from Angeles Temple in Los Angeles and through numerous "lighthouses" that sprung up across the nation.

North American Pentecostals and Evangelicals for many years were quite gun shy to terms such as *social concern* and *social justice* for a few reasons. One was the fear of losing a spiritual edge by embracing a "social gospel," which was identified with the notions of Walter Rauschenbusch and similar post-Millennialist theologies. The second reason was a fear that such an emphasis would diminish the salvific and pneumatological priorities of the gospel. And third, for some it was simply too politically volatile and smacked a bit of socialism.

It seems that Pentecostals, like many Evangelicals, for a season at least, were passionate about preaching the good news and calling people to repentance and meaningful relationship with Christ. We poured much into giving people hope. But as Baptist pastor DeForest Soaries has said, "People need *hope,* but they also need *help.* If you only give them *help* with no *hope,* they might have full stomachs but they may still commit suicide."[5] Help will feed their bodies; hope will feed their souls.

In their book *Global Pentecostalism: The New Face of Christian Social Engagement,* Donald E. Miller and Tetsunao Yamamori identify "Progressive Pentecostals" as "a movement of Christians who claim to be inspired by the

Holy Spirit and the life of Jesus and seek to holistically address the spiritual, physical, and social needs of people in their community."[6] From extensive research, Miller reports that since 1980, Pentecostal-Charismatics have contributed over 2.3 billion dollars and assisted 250 million people with goods and services in over 100 countries.[7]

Globally, however, in several other countries outside the United States, Pentecostalism has not been nearly as reluctant to embrace the more social dimensions of the gospel. In Brazil, Chile, and other Latin American regions, for instance, Pentecostals have incorporated ministry efforts that have been truly holistic, extending not only to places of worship but also into systems of education, agri-business, and other environments.[8] Much has been written of the undeniable social lift brought to vast regions of the disenfranchised because of the impact of Pentecostalism.

Compassionate Pentecostalism

In a *Time* magazine article on the Latino Reformation, Elizabeth Dias wrote, "Music and sermons alone are not enough to draw people. A hungry person, the saying goes, has no ears."[9] Latino churches around the world engage in a multiplicity of ways in serving the needs of the disadvantaged. In the same article, Heber Paredes Sr. said, "We never let people stay in need. We are not going to be able to sleep if we know a family needs food."[10]

Two of the most long-standing social efforts among Pentecostals have been Teen Challenge and Latin American Childcare. Established in 1958 by Assemblies of God minister David Wilkerson, Teen Challenge has grown to become the oldest, largest, and most successful drug rehabilitation program of its kind, with over 170 centers in the United States and one thousand centers worldwide in over eighty countries. It records an unrivaled 70 percent success rate, as compared to a 1–15 percent success rate among similar secular programs.

Founded by Pentecostals in 1963, Latin American Childcare is the largest integrated network of Evangelical schools in Latin America and the Caribbean. It incorporates over three hundred compassionate projects that affect more than one hundred thousand children in twenty-one countries.

Social action has "very definitely" taken on a new role among Pentecostals and Pentecostal churches in the United States today, according to Assemblies of God national leader George Wood. He oversaw a sweeping missional step at the organization's national convention in Orlando. Wood says, "The AG in 2009 added 'compassion' as the fourth element for its reason for being—in recognition that Jesus came to glorify God (worship), save the lost, make disciples, but also serve human need."[11]

Different Gospels?

There still exists today a spiritual and emotional divide between many black and white Christians over these "different" or "differing" gospels. Those who favor the "social gospel" feel that the salvation-focused gospel too often overlooks present and pressing needs in people's lives. All the while, salvation-focused believers feel that the "social gospel" compromised tending to things eternal while focusing "only" or primarily on temporal needs.

Ultimately, however, through neglect by some Evangelicals (even well-meaning ones), "Jesus" too often was left "in prison" and alone and unvisited or was shunned while "hungry" and left to starve. Even during the civil rights movement of the 1960s, many Christians allowed personal prejudices to blur their view of people, such as Dr. Martin Luther King Jr., and how God was using him and others like him to confront injustice. The Latino Reformation today is doing something quite different in the church; it is "introducing" MLK to Billy Graham and helping him and others like him walk side by side in ministry, causing righteousness and justice to unite or reunite. Latino Christ-followers are emerging rapidly as the most pro-life, pro-family, pro-biblical-justice faith demographic in the United States.

Mercy and truth have met.

Righteousness and peace have kissed.

(Psalm 85:10, God's Word)

It is time for the message of mercy and the confrontation of truth to reconnect; we must introduce Billy Graham to Martin Luther King Jr. by virtue of our passion, our conviction, and our practices as a church.

With this, the question arises: Did MLK and Graham ever meet in real life, and if so, what must that discussion and those interactions have been like?

Billy and Mike

Amid the renewed racial tensions in America, it seems that both white and black pastors as well as Christians of all ethnicities would be wise to take the lead from the relational example of Billy Graham and Martin Luther King Jr. Graham and King became close friends in the late 1950s and early 60s. "As their friendship grew, Dr. King asked Mr. Graham to call him by his nickname. 'His father,' explains Graham, 'who was called Big Mike, called him Little Mike. He asked me to call him just plain Mike.'"[12]

In 1953, with America full of racial tension and anxieties, Billy Graham chose to do something then socially unthinkable: "he held a crusade in Chattanooga, Tennessee, where thousands of men, women, and children of all races sat together and worshiped the Lord."[13] But this did not occur without a challenge.

In the early fifties, it was common for ropes to be used in the South to separate the white section (usually at the front of the auditorium) from the black section (at the back). When Graham walked into the auditorium the first night of the crusade, he saw that the dividing ropes were up. He asked the head usher to remove them. The usher refused. His son, Franklin, recalls, "So Daddy went down there and did it himself, and a lot of the churches pulled out of the meetings because of my father's position on standing against the segregation."

Never again did Graham preach a crusade with any racial restrictions on seating.[14]

Of this season of ministry and justice efforts, Graham observed:

Civil rights were very much in the forefront in America during the 1960s and early 1970s. As the issue unfolded, I sometimes found myself under fire from both sides, extreme conservatives castigating me for doing too much and extreme liberals blaming me for not doing enough. In reality, both groups tended to stand aloof from our evangelistic Crusades, but those people who actively supported us understood very well our commitment to doing what we could through our evangelism to end the blight of racism.[15]

Graham and King at the Garden

A couple of years after Chattanooga, Graham had been preaching nightly to thousands at Madison Square Garden in New York City. He became concerned, however, since the audience was overwhelmingly white. At the suggestion of a colleague, he conferred with an African American pastor, Howard Jones, for advice. Jones recommended that Graham "take his message to the streets of New York."[16]

Graham went to Harlem and "preached at Salem Methodist Church [a black congregation] to thousands. The next week, he went to Brooklyn. . . . Prominent singer Ethel Waters attended the event and rededicated her life to Christ."[17] Graham invited people in these areas to come to the Garden for his meetings, and many did.

Soon thereafter, "Graham even invited his good friend Dr. Martin Luther King Jr. to attend one of the events." King sat right next to Graham at the event and just before the sermon, he prayed,

We thank Thee this evening for the marvelous things which have
been done in this city through the dynamic preaching of this great
evangelist. We ask Thee, O God, to continue blessing him. Give him
continued power and authority that as we listen to him tonight, grant
that our hearts and spirits will be open to the divine inflow.[18]

Amid a number of experiments and bold steps toward integration, Graham continued to consult with MLK. Graham said, "Martin Luther King
suggested to me that I stay in the stadiums in the South and hold integrated
meetings, because he was probably going to take to the streets. He said, 'I'll
probably stay in the streets and I might get killed in the streets. . . . You will be
able to do things I can't do and I can do some things you can't do, but we're
after the same objective.'"[19]

Martin in Puerto Rico

In 1962, six years before his assassination, MLK traveled to Puerto Rico to give
a few speeches. One of them was at the Inter-American University on "The
Future of Integration." This portion of his speech speaks to the central passion
of his life, leadership, and ministry:

For God is not interested merely in the freedom of black men, and
brown men, and yellow men; God is interested in the freedom of the
whole human race, and the creation of a society where all men will live
together as brothers. And I believe that by living this philosophy, by
using every resource of energy that we can develop to pare down the
old order, but at the same time maintaining an attitude of love, and
refusing to use violence, we will be able to bring into being this new
day, and it will be a great and marvelous day when all of God's children
will be able to live together as brothers. And so, to paraphrase the words

of John Oxenham, the high nation climbs the high way and the low nation gropes the low, and in between the rest drift to and fro, but every nation decides which way its soul shall go.[20]

The Same Message of Love in Different Colors

In the 1950s Graham was preaching that there is "no excuse ever for hatred. No excuse ever for bigotry. We've got to love as God loved us."[21]

MLK preached, "We don't need any guns. We don't need any bullets. We don't need any physical ammunition. We have a power. All we need is to pick up the ammunition of love, take in our hands the weapons of justice, then put on the 'breastplate of righteousness' and to hold on to God and just start marching."[22]

The Black, the White, and the Brown

We believe that God wants to use the Latino church, to use Hispanic Christians, to help bring healing to the divide that exists in America between blacks and whites. Put simply, God wants to use the brown to help heal the black and the white.

Latinos have walked through a challenging season in America. Although they are in a land of immigrants, some of the more nonloving "passions" aroused in recent years could make them feel unwanted, rejected, and even abandoned.

Ultimately, our capacity to love as individuals must grow if the divides are going to be overcome and if real racial reconciliation is to occur. The answer is in the gospel of Jesus Christ and the transformation he can bring to the human heart, to the soul. While we need legislation, this alone cannot heal our land and fix our social divides. It must come from a deeper place, from the soul.

Bernice King, the youngest daughter of MLK, was only five years old when her father was assassinated. She has said, "I think both Dr. Graham and my father were trying to make the world a better place. They were different, obviously, in their style and their approach, but I think their heart and their goal was the same."[23]

FEED THE FIRE
Questions to Ignite Growth and Change

1. What stories or memories do you have of Martin Luther King Jr.? In what ways has he impacted your life and faith?

2. What stories or memories do you or your family have of Billy Graham? How has he impacted your life and faith?

3. In the way they practiced their faith, what do MLK and Graham have in common?

4. In the way they practiced their faith, how were MLK and Graham different?

5. Which is most important as a Christian: sharing your faith or sharing your food? Explain.

6. How can Christians balance **hope** and **help** in living out their faith and serving others?

7. Could God use the brown to help bring together the black and the white? How so? Where could it begin?

A Latino Pope?

The Francis Effect

> This is the fire of the Holy Spirit. If the Church does
> not receive this fire . . . it becomes a cold or lukewarm
> Church, incapable of giving life.
> —Pope Francis, Saint Peter's Square,
> August 14, 2016

The most extraordinary leadership event in history, signaling the effect of the church's move to the global south was, arguably, the selection of Jorge Mario Bergoglio as pope of the Roman Catholic Church. On March 13, 2013, this newly appointed ecclesial leader chose a papal name in honor of Saint Francis of Assisi. That day, Francis became the *first* Jesuit pope, the *first* pope from the Americas, the *first* from the Southern Hemisphere, the *first* non-European pope since the eighth-century Syrian Gregory III, and the *first* Latino pope.[1]

Born in Buenos Aires, Argentina, Francis (that is, young Jorge) worked for a brief time as a chemical technologist and nightclub bouncer before entering seminary. He served as a priest for several years, and from 1973 to 1979 became the provincial secretary of the Society of Jesus in Argentina. In 1998, he became the archbishop of Buenos Aires, and by 2001 he was named a cardinal by Pope John Paul II. A papal enclave elected Bergoglio as pope on March 13, 2013.[2]

From the start, Francis made changes once he arrived in Rome. His manner, style, decisions, and nature as a leader made an immediate impact felt around the world. He personified the *Passio Dei* and exhibited not only a passion for God but also a compassion for people. He regularly broke the standards of papal decorum, often walking out of security-managed constraints and right into crowds and reaching out to hurting people. Despite his regal privileges and afforded accommodations, he chooses to reside in the Domus Sanctae Marthae guesthouse rather than in the papal apartments of the apostolic palace always used by his predecessors.

Francis brought his Latino-bred collectivist nature and warmth to his new role in Rome, insisting that the Catholic Church be more open and welcoming. While progressive in his manner, he has remained quite traditional in his values and views of church life regarding abortion, euthanasia, contraception, homosexuality, marriage, ordination of women, and priestly celibacy. However, he opposes consumerism, supports action on climate change, and worked to restore diplomatic relations between the United States and Cuba.

"Latin America . . . accounts for 40 percent of the world's Catholics. . . . According to the *Annuarium Statisticum Ecclesiae*—the statistical yearbook of the Catholic church—and [according to] the World Christian Database, between 1910 and 2010 the total number of Catholics in the region grew by 700 percent, just behind the population. . . . Non-Catholic Christians (a category that includes most Protestants, including Pentecostals) grew by 5,500 percent." Beyond these statistics, however, was an even larger demographic. The "'double affiliated'—baptized Catholics who attend church elsewhere—grew by 17,000 percent," posing a major issue for the Catholic church.[3]

Not only is the Latino Reformation now in full swing; the leader of the Catholic Church, for the first time in history, is a Latino himself, an Argentinian, in fact. But what impact will the Latino Reformation continue to have? That influence is being felt now among Protestants and Catholics, as in parts of Latin America, the Catholic Church is copying some of the practices, worship forms, and approaches of their sister Pentecostal churches.

The "Francis Effect": The Significance of a Latino Pope

The emergence of Pope Francis is a seismic sociological mile marker for Latino Christianity in general. It holds great significance. Even for those Latinos who no longer identify with Catholicism, this appointment is a harbinger that should not be overlooked by any serious student of faith and global dynamics. There are several significant factors to consider, herein referred to as "the Francis effect."[4] While these may not all materialize, there are certainly arguable considerations.

Francis Effect 1: The Shifting of a Global Ecclesial Leadership Mantle or Role to a Latino

This effect is not an isolated phenomenon of Roman Catholicism but representative of a global change. Realize and recognize that one of the most conservative and "unchangeable" groups in the world has just made a massive change in its selection of a leader. This decision broke another glass ceiling and will affect the global church in the aspect that Protestant denominations will see some similar changes.

Catholics were first in this respect, but they will doubtlessly not be last. What other denominational "mantles" will we see pass to a Latino in the next five to ten years? Will American-based Pentecostal denominations be next? Also, what governmental positions will make similar changes? How long will it be, for instance, until we elect a Latino president in the United States?

Francis Effect 2: A More Personable Pope May Tend Toward a More Personable Perception of Christianity and of Catholicism

One Latin American Jesuit said, "This pope emphasizes important things, like God, mercy and the poor: he doesn't just talk about the Church." When asked to respond to the statement " 'Pope Francis has inspired me to feel closer to the Catholic church' . . . 59% of all Latin Americans and 73% of all Catholics" agreed that the pope had done so. A humanized pope will likely make for more humanized and approachable forms of Catholicism in various contextualized examples.

Francis Effect 3: The Election of a Latino Pope Could Lead to a Much-Sought-After Renaissance Period for the Catholic Church

This, however, will take some major changes since the "long-term erosion" of Catholicism has been so significant on so many fronts. The changes Francis is making include (1) his new and more open style and manner; (2) his underscoring of key issues and concerns among the people of Latin America including poverty, human rights, and social justice; and (3) his recognition and praise for the Pentecostal vitality present in Latin America and Africa. These are in contrast to his predecessors, and the outcomes of these initiatives are yet to be seen but should not be underestimated.

Francis Effect 4: The Exporting of Francis from Argentina to the Helm of Roman Catholicism Is Symbolic of a Paradigmatic Change from Viewing Latin America Primarily as a Missionary Destination to, Now, a Missionary Exporter or Sending Agency

Daniel Levine notes that for decades Protestant churches from America and other parts of the world had to export pastors and resources to South America. Today, Pentecostal and Protestant churches in these very regions are "exporting leaders and expanding their presence elsewhere in the global south." For example, *"Igreja Universal do Reino de Deus* (Universal Church of the Kingdom of God), founded in Brazil in 1977, is now active throughout Latin America, Africa, Europe, and the United States."

Francis Effect 5: Since His Election, Francis Seems Determined to Reform the Vatican Much More Than His Predecessors

Levine notes that Francis has specifically "[addressed] clerical sexual abuse and ongoing financial scandals" in the church and has reorganized "Vatican finances to increase transparency and accountability, [and] removed some notable tradi-tionalists from key positions." He has also "reached out to victims of sexual abuse and promised an end to cover-ups" in these types of cases. While he may not ever "change formal Vatican positions on homosexual behavior, same-sex marriage, divorce, contraception, abortion, and the like," unlike his predecessors he strikes a more conciliatory and understanding tone in the public debate.

Francis Effect 6: Francis Has the Opportunity to Help an Old Church Discover How to Better Function in a New World

"The Catholic Church in Latin America exists in a very different world from the one in which most of its leaders were raised and educated." Today's world consists of people who are far more used to personal freedoms and powers, who "are mobile and educated," and who have many options and access to powerful technologies and various types of media. Theology can pour in their directions from many more places than just a pulpit. They are influenced by global brands, dynamics, and ideologies via cultural trends and a diversity of con-sumer goods. These constantly challenge and affect their views and values.

The Catholic Church's challenge, along with all churches for that matter, is how to navigate the changing environment faithfully and effectively. The previous two popes before Francis underlined the need to renew discipline and unity in the church. Benedict decried the effects of a growing secularization and globalization.

Francis Effect 7: Francis Is Leveling the Playing Fields Within Catholicism and Moving the Church away from Euro-Centrism

Although Francis did not emerge from "the liberation theology tradition, he has been more open to it than his predecessors." For example, "he welcomed Peruvian theologian Gustavo Gutiérrez, one of the movement's major figures, to the Vatican." Francis "has also moved to internationalize the Vatican's gov-ernment, the Roman Curia," by giving more of a voice at the table to leaders beyond Italy and Europe in his "a council of prelates (with a majority from the global south) to advise him directly." By virtue of his heritage and experience, Latin America has taken a major step ahead in leadership and influence in the future decisions of the Catholic Church. Will all the efforts of Francis and company be successful at "[reversing] the long-term erosion" within Catholicism? This remains to be seen. However, this new pope is arguably bringing change that is desired by many.

Francis in America: Papal Confrontations

When Pope Francis was welcomed by President Obama at the White House for his first visit on September 23, 2015, the president introduced him as "the first" of several: As the *first* pope from the Americas, the *first* pope from South America, the *first* Latino pope, and the *first* pope to release an encyclical on Twitter.[5]

When the pope came to America, it should be noted that he came as a Latino missionary from Argentina by way of Rome. His tribute was more than customary or ceremonial; it was by nature more missional. In other words, he came with an agenda. By only the second formal sentence Pope Francis spoke in America, he had already confronted something in this nation: our challenges with immigration. He said,

> Mr. President, I am deeply grateful for your welcome in the name of all Americans. *As a son of an immigrant family, I am happy to be a guest in this country, which was largely built by such families.*[6] (emphasis added)

Pope Francis challenged the church in the United States to welcome immigrants, to love their "neighbor" more fully. Later on that same day, Francis addressed the bishops from all over America gathered in Washington, DC, to meet with him. Once again, he challenged them regarding the issue of immigrants coming to America. He said,

I ask you to excuse me if in some way I am pleading my own case. The Church in the United States knows like few others the hopes present in the hearts of these "pilgrims" [that is, immigrants]. From the beginning you have learned their languages, promoted their cause, made their contributions your own, defended their rights, helped them to prosper, and kept alive the flame of their faith. Even today, no American institution does more for immigrants than your Christian communities. Now you are facing this stream of Latin immigration which affects many of your dioceses. Not only as the Bishop of Rome, but also as a pastor from the South, I feel the need to thank and encourage you. Perhaps it will not be easy for you to look into their soul; perhaps you will be challenged by their diversity. But know that they also possess resources meant to be shared. So do not be afraid to welcome them. Offer them the warmth of the love of Christ and you will unlock the mystery of their heart. I am certain that, as so often in the past, these people will enrich America and its Church.[7]

Pope Francis empathized with Latin American immigrants in his speech given at Independence Hall in Philadelphia. At this address, Francis noted that among the group gathered that day were "members of America's large Hispanic population, as well as representatives of recent immigrants to the United States." He affirmed the immigrants present, noting that they had come "to this country at great personal cost, in the hope of building a new life." He urged them not to let themselves be "discouraged by . . . hardships." He reminded them that they, "like those who came here before [them] . . . bring many gifts to this nation." He urged them to "never be ashamed of [their] traditions" nor to "forget the lessons . . . learned from [their] elders."[8] His affirmations continued,

You are called to be responsible citizens . . . and to contribute fruitfully . . . to the life of the communities in which you live. . . . By

contributing your gifts, you will not only find your place here, you
will help to renew society from within.[9]

He ended his talk that day by reminding the people gathered at Independence Hall to "not forget what took place [there] over two centuries ago." He reminded them of the "Declaration [of Independence] which proclaimed that all men and women are created equal, that they are endowed by their Creator with certain inalienable rights and that governments exist in order to protect and defend those rights."[10]

Pope Francis called Catholics in the United States to avoid apathy and to engage a more joyous faith—to love God more fully. At the Basilica of the National Shrine of the Immaculate Conception in Washington, DC, he urged the congregation gathered to

> rejoice in the Lord always! I say it again, rejoice! These are striking
> words, words which impact our lives. Paul tells us to rejoice; he
> practically orders us to rejoice. This command resonates with the
> desire we all have for a fulfilling life, a meaningful life, a joyful life.[11]

Bridges to Pentecostals and Evangelicals?

Within a year of Francis's inauguration as pope, he made an unprecedented visit to a Pentecostal church in Italy and apologized for their past poor treatment by Catholics. *Christianity Today* reported, "During his July 28 [2014] visit to the Evangelical Church of Reconciliation in Caserta, the pope apologized for the past persecution of Pentecostals under Italy's fascist regime, which did not allow them to practice their faith." Francis said, "Among those who persecuted and denounced Pentecostals, almost as if they were crazy people trying to ruin the race, there were also Catholics." He added, "I am the pastor of Catholics, and I ask your forgiveness."[12]

Some Italian Pentecostals, however, are more skeptical of the overtures of the new pope than are many Western ones. "'There is much naiveté and superficiality,' Italian church planter Leonardo De Chirico wrote in a blog post."[13]

But the challenge of building bridges with Pentecostal Evangelicals is but one faced by the Catholic Church. There are others that Francis has before him.

The Catholic Challenges

The Percentage of Hispanics Who Call Themselves "Catholic" Is Decreasing

According to a 2013 Pew Research Center survey, from 2010 to 2013, the number of Hispanics who call themselves "Catholic" dropped 12 percentage points, from 67 percent to 55 percent. The survey also found that today "nearly one-in-four Hispanic adults (24%) are now *former* Catholics," while "22% are Protestant . . . and 18% are religiously unaffiliated."[14] "Enrique Pumar, the chair of the sociology department at The Catholic University of America, explained [that] . . . the first (reason) is that there are other Christian churches that are making a concerted effort to basically practice and evangelize people in Latin America. The Catholic Church no longer has a monopoly. Today, people have options." It has now "become acceptable within the Hispanic community to switch denominations."[15]

The Percentage of Catholics in the United States Who Are Hispanic Is Increasing

Hispanics continue to make up an increasing percentage and large share of US Catholics, but at the same time the percentage of Hispanics who self-identify as Catholics is declining. As of 2013, according to Pew Research, "one-third (33%) of all U.S. Catholics were Hispanic."[16]

The reason these contrasting trends are possible among Latinos and Catholics is the rapid growth of the overall Hispanic population in the United States, "having increased from 12.5% of the total U.S. population in 2000" to 17.6 percent in 2015. Note this: at the current rate of growth, we are approaching a day "when a majority of Catholics in the United States will be Hispanic, even though the majority of Hispanics might no longer be Catholic."[17]

The Number of Younger Hispanic Catholics in the United States Is Decreasing

"While the decline in Catholic affiliation is occurring among multiple age groups, it is more pronounced among younger generations of Hispanics. . . . Fewer than half of Hispanics under age 30 are Catholic (45%), compared with about two-thirds of those ages 50 and older (64%)."[18]

More Hispanic Catholics Are Embracing Pentecostal Practices

The Latino American experience is becoming more charismatic, as they are more open to the *pneuma,* the moving of the Holy Spirit. These groups are moving Christ to the center of their faith experience—less Mary, more Jesus. The movement is more toward biblical truth where people engage the Word on a daily basis. Latinos are facilitating and leading the Evangelical transformation of Catholicism. Latinos in Latin America and in the United States primarily lead this new Catholic Evangelicalism, a sort of hybrid form.

Hispanic Christians Desire Family-Friendly Ministries, Communities, and Worship Experiences

A *Time* article reported, "The Catholic church now has 4,800 parishes with Latino programs of various kinds across the U.S. According to the U.S. Conference of Catholic Bishops, up to half of Latino Catholics in America are expressing their faith much as the evangelical community does—praying with hands raised, speaking in tongues, expecting the miraculous."[19] There has been a resurgence of the Catholic Charismatic Renewal.

Yet a couple of major challenges remain: (1) "Only 15% of all new priests ordained in the U.S. are Latino," and (2) Hispanic Catholics desire "very flexible, very family-oriented" church structures and systems, something not usually attributed to Catholicism. If these challenges are not addressed, the

Catholic Church "will continue to lose a significant number of Hispanic Catholics to other religious groups, mostly Pentecostals."[20]

A Prodigal?

On the Sunday before the conclave of bishops—those who chose the new leader (Pope Francis) of the Catholic church in 2013—began, the gospel reading in Catholic churches around the world happened to be the parable of the prodigal son (see Luke 15), the tale of a spoiled heir who takes his inheritance and wastes it, only to be forgiven by his father and taken back in. That week many cardinals used the scripture as an opportunity to call straying Catholics back to the fold. A *Time* magazine article cited another possibility: Francis may have seen it differently, since perhaps "the church itself has been prodigal, and now may be the time for it to find its way back to its people."[21]

FEED THE FIRE
Questions to Ignite Growth and Change

1. How has Catholicism changed in recent years?
2. In what ways has Pope Francis impacted the Catholic Church and culture in general?
3. What do you think the "Francis effect" will be?
4. Are Catholics misunderstood today by Protestants? Explain.
5. What are some of the opportunities Catholics face today?
6. What are some of the challenges Catholics face today?
7. How are Pentecostalism and the Charismatic movement affecting the Catholic Church today?

8

Race and Grace

I wanted to know what people of color have been
through so I could understand how they think, feel,
and act.

—Pastor J. Don George,
Calvary Assembly, Irving, Texas

Peru has become my (Robert's) home away from home during the past five
years. During that time my wife, Pamela, and I have traveled there and to
other parts of South America several times, primarily partnering with pastors
such as Guillermo and Milagros Aguayo from Lima. They remind us somewhat of a younger James and Shirley Dobson, as God is blessing their transformative ministry to Hispanic families all throughout South America. This
ministry, more of a movement, is called *Salvemos a la Familia* (Save the Family), and it is producing beautiful life change throughout Latin America and
beyond.

In parts of the world where families are struggling desperately with issues
such as machismo, domestic abuse, incest, and poverty, Salvemos a la Familia
is bringing hope and healing to many homes. Some of the most inspiring and
anointing teachings we have received on family life have come from the
Aguayos, from their ministry and resources.

On one trip to Lima not long ago, Pamela and I were enjoying a meal with
Guillermo, Milagros, and their young-adult children. As we shared the time
together, it suddenly occurred to me that we had a rare opportunity. We could
either use the time to simply talk about our own lives and tell a story or two . . .

or we could ask a few questions and might actually learn something. So I ventured out and asked, "Guillermo, since you and your family are all here, do you mind if I ask all of you a couple of questions, just a few things I am interested to know from you?"

Guillermo quickly obliged.

"What are some things that missionaries and ministers from America assume or get wrong when they come to visit you here in Peru?" I asked.

Without a moment's hesitation, Guillermo turned to me and responded with clarity and passion, "That the United States is the center of the church and of the revelation of God!"

The immediacy of Guillermo's response took me aback just a bit. It was clear that our host had been waiting, seemingly for years, for someone from the United States to ask him this kind of question. It was answered not only with conviction but also frustration. While our hosts were as usual exceedingly gracious to us that day, I felt as if I got a peek into a part of their souls and felt just a bit of their angst.

We unpacked these comments over the next hour or so. It was a moment I will not soon forget, as if Guillermo allowed me to see a few things through his personal lens. There is "a time for every purpose under heaven," says Ecclesiastes 3:1, NKJV, and this for me was certainly not "a time to speak" but "a time to keep silence" (verse 7, NKJV) and listen. In those moments I came to recognize something I had simply missed for many years: my Americanized worldview included some measures of bias and entitlement. It seems a certain air of "American exceptionalism" and "entitlement" had preceded me and my visits; I carried some of it myself.

Somebody Else's Lens

One thing our divided world could really use right now is for each of us to pick up someone else's "eyeglasses" and take a moment to try to look through them.

In other words, a little effort to consider someone else's worldview and just a few of the influences that have shaped that person could do a world of good in your neighborhood or community. But you have to care enough to pick those glasses up and actually try hard enough to focus and look at the world, if but for a moment, through the person's eyes. If we would do this, we would soon find out some surprising things.

- **The way** *someone else* **sees the world is probably quite different from the way** *you* **do.** While we may never have considered ourselves to be prejudiced or racist, the truth is that through the process of enculturation we all have tendencies toward certain biases, some often narrow-minded and unfair but also quite natural to come by given our contextual circumstances. The truth is that the last person to see your blind spots is usually *you*.

- **If you can try to** *see a bit* **of what they see, you will start to** *feel a bit* **of what they feel.** This is the beauty of the Incarnation and how Jesus came to look through our life lens. Dick Foth describes the gospel this way: "Jesus says, 'I'm going to leave *my place;* I'm going to come to *your place;* I'm going to take *your place;* and, then we are going to go to *my place.*'" Christ entered our world in part to identify with our struggles, weaknesses, and temptations (see Hebrews 4:15). This helped him become our chief advocate.

- **Sincere questions and focused listening to the answers are the best ways to look through someone else's lens.** In order to tap your own interest and curiosity, before you ask someone a question, ask yourself a few: *I wonder what it would be like to see the world through their life and experiences? I wonder how their family, race, or ethnic heritage has shaped their view of the world? I wonder what their highest hopes are? I wonder what their deepest hurts and frustrations are? I wonder how I might better understand, serve, and befriend them?*

Philippians 2:4 says, "Do not merely look out for your own personal interests, but also for the interests of others" (NASB). In order to be interest*ing,* you must be interest*ed.* You will gain more friends in three minutes by getting interested in other people than you will in three months of trying to get them interested in you. The few minutes I took to show interest in the Aguayos and their perspective opened my eyes to a world of new realities that changed my view and the way I feel in my heart.

Immigration Fears

We also live in a perilous time in the United States and other places due to racial tensions, regional divisions, political unrest, and terrorism. While the Bible challenges us to have a faith that opens our doors to the helpless, homeless, and hurting, parents and other family members more and more feel a responsibility to protect their children. Thus, Christians face a difficult question today: *How can I love my neighbor in today's world and yet still protect my children?*

Dr. Samuel Pagan notes, "We need to do something about our border. But the key issue for doing so should not be race but rather security."[1] And along those lines, Republican political commentator Alex Castellanos recently said, "We all lock our doors at night not because we hate the people outside, but because we love the people inside."[2]

In considering the difficult question of loving your neighbor and protecting your children, we always have to be suspect of fear, Gabe Lyons, the founder of Q Ideas, cautions. Fear is a bully and a poor motivation for life and relationships. While it will raise tensions, it will not raise up confident sons and daughters. In fact, John wrote in 1 John 4 that the remedy to fear is "perfect love." He confirmed, "There is no fear in love." Fear is the antithesis of love. Fear deceives, paralyzes, and divides us. Love unites. And love is so powerful that "perfect love drives out fear." Fear will fade as we realize just how perfectly loved by God we truly are.

"While we want to be responsible with our families," Lyons urges, "we have to be careful not to let that drive ministry decisions. Often God shows up after we take those risks and those steps. Our families benefit when they see us willing to step out in our faith." One of these ways is in how we treat people who are different from us: Do we do so with or without grace?[3]

Graceless

Unfortunately, when it comes to interacting with people of different races, nationalities, or even religions, history has shown that sin and selfishness have led to many unkindnesses. Over the years, so many people have suffered personally, emotionally, and even physically due to racism, prejudice, and words best described as *graceless.*

Graceless moments and graceless people: they have a way of sucking the life right out of us, don't they? They put the clamps down on our spirits and keep us from breathing. Inconsiderate. Disrespectful. Out to hurt. Gracelessness always comes at the most inopportune times. It snatches all notions of faith, hope, and love right out of us and replaces them with doubt, suspicion, and anger.

Paul knew all about graceless moments and people. Even though he was the trailblazing pioneer of the Corinthian church, this particular group also brought him much heartache. Despite the fact that he had been the first to bring the gospel to Corinth, the Christians there had fallen prey to more than one smooth-talking critic during his absence. The Corinthian Christians frequently ran high on expectations and low on grace as it concerned their founding pastor.

A closer look at this particular congregation, including their attitude toward Paul, reveals much about what happens when we choose to live *without* grace.

Without grace, labels abound. The Corinthian Christians loved to label. Strung hard around Paul's neck were long-distance labels that read "Noneloquent Speaker," "Unpopular," "Pushy Letter-writer," "Bold in Print—Weak in Presence." These labels were types of prejudices in their own right.[4]

Labels can be powerful, powerfully accurate and powerfully painful. We tend to place all kinds of labels on people every day. Even in the church.

Whether from racial or religious bias, when we label a person we combine two devastating forces. First, we judge and measure according to our own set of scales and balances (see Matthew 7:1–2). Second, in addition to judging, we give up on hope. In effect, we say to the person we label, "This negative term describes the way you are. You *are* this way, you have *always* been this way, and you will *always* be this way. I have no hope that you might change. I will view you through this label lens and always think of you in light of it. I have you all figured out. Any questions?"

Latino Labels

I (Samuel) have found that non-Hispanics in the United States, Europe, and other areas all too often have misconceptions about Hispanics. A lack of grace is often evidenced by views that non-Hispanics have about Hispanics. Often these are based on myths that develop through a chain of racial gossip or a bad experience someone has had, either of which then gets turned into a propagated stereotype. Some prejudices come by personal ignorance, some by foolishness, and some by political posturing and vitriol. Here are some of the most common myths or labels assigned to Latinos.

Myth 1: Hispanics Are a Monolithic Voting Bloc

Counter: Due to the diversity of the different immigrant groups that compose the Latino demographic, this statement simply is not true. As mentioned earlier, Latinos are actually not a race; rather, they represent an ethnicity, a composite of three races. There is the Cuban American experience, the Puerto Rican American experience, and the Mexican American experience, which represent the three largest groups (Mexicans first and Puerto Ricans second), each one unique.

The politics, cultural dynamics, historical context, and the socioeconomic backgrounds along with the fact that the majority of individuals that migrated were from Cuba (post-1959) were all concerns primarily before the 1980 migration. Those who first migrated were the business and the educated class, and they gravitated toward the Republican establishment. Thus, Cubans, until the Millennial generation, voted primarily Republican. Puerto Ricans voted primarily Democrat. Mexicans were primarily Democrat, but they are split, especially in Texas where there is a strong conservative Mexican movement.

Myth 2: Hispanics Are All Democrats

Counter: Latinos are not a monolithic voting constituency. In fact, 44 percent of Hispanics voted for George W. Bush in 2004, 27 percent voted for Mitt Romney in 2012, and 29 percent voted for Donald Trump in 2016.[5] More and more Latinos are registering as Independent registered voters. I (Sam) predict that by 2024, 50 percent will be registered Independent voters.

Myth 3: Hispanics Refuse to Assimilate or Acculturate

Counter: Latinos actually assimilate at a faster rate than the Italian Americans of the late 1800s and early 1900s did. Studies have indicated Latinos actually embrace and demonstrate proficiencies in the English vernacular and embrace the major threads and components of the American cultural experience at a faster rate than immigrants in the early 1900s, so it's perception versus reality. It is not only a misnomer but also a mischaracterization of the facts. Latinos do assimilate, but it is more a process of acculturation than assimilation. Latinos likewise tend to maintain or preserve the Spanish vernacular as well as the practices and customs from their motherlands in ways that are more significant after two or three generations in comparison to Italian Americans and Irish Americans.

Myth 4: Hispanics Are All Catholics

Counter: Latinos are not all Catholics. In fact, the fastest-growing denominational group among Latinos is the Evangelicals. Latino Catholicism actually
continues to decrease in America due to the growth of Latino Evangelicalism.
So, more and more Latinos are converting to Evangelicalism from Catholicism,
and the bridge is the Catholic Charismatic experience. The vast majority of
Latino Catholics who become Latino Evangelicals become Latino Pentecostals. Most non-Catholic Latinos are part of the Charismatic experience.

The majority of Latino Catholics (52 percent), according to Pew Research,
are Latino Catholic Charismatics.[6] This means they are open to the supernatural things and manifestations of the Holy Spirit via the conduit of a prayer
language, praying for the sick, and so forth.

Myth 5: Hispanics Lack Leadership

Counter: We have our versions of Martin Luther King Jr. Because of the diversity of the Latino community in comparison to the African American community, the idea of one leader is not practical, nor can it happen. This is because
of the diversity of Mexicans, Puerto Ricans, Dominicans—the native-land
diversity and the different optics that guide every single community. The idea
of having one voice speaking on behalf of the entire community does not fall
within the bounds of reality.

In fact, there also has been a lack of one unified leadership in the civil
rights movement. The African American community has been divided between the followers of Dr. King, of Malcolm X, of the Black Panthers, and so
forth. Dr. King did emerge as the most recognized figure of the movement.

We Latinos likewise have a number of viable leaders in our community:
within the business world, Hollywood, media, culture, and politics. We have
those in government like Marco Rubio and Ted Cruz. As it pertains to media,
we have a number of amazing directors and actors who have emerged with
great prominence and presence: the Jennifer Lopezes, the Ricky Martins, the

Mark Anthonys, the Pit Bulls, the Lin Manuel Mirandas (of the musical *Hamilton*), and so forth. And in the church arena, God is doing much through the NHCLC and other groups.

Myth 6: Hispanics Represent an Unchangeable Deliverable Constituency

Counter: While President Clinton won the Latino vote when he ran for president by a 72 percent to 21 percent split in 1996, President Obama won it by a 71 percent to 27 percent split in 2008. However, although she lost the election in 2016, Hillary Clinton won the Latino vote but by a smaller margin than Obama at a 65 percent to 29 percent split. There seems to be a constituency movement or change that is taking place.

Myth 7: Hispanics Desire Amnesty

Counter: Not all Latinos desire amnesty. In fact, in 2014 a Gallup poll showed that while 75 percent of Latino immigrants approved it, the issue was almost split among Hispanics born in the United States.[7]

Without Grace, Comparisons Emerge

Early in the history of the Corinthian church, her parishioners drew lines in the sand and began to choose sides. They developed distinct biases and prejudices. Instead of being in awe of the person of Christ, they chose to be awestruck by the personalities who sought to represent him.

Playing favorites, some said, "I am on Paul's side; he's our founder!" Others said, "I am with Apollos all the way; he can really preach!" Still others, seeking to out-awe them all, would pontificate, "Well, I am of Christ himself!" (authors' paraphrases of 1 Corinthians 3:4, 23).

One of Paul's first written confrontations with the Corinthians was over this very matter.

I'm completely frustrated by your unspiritual dealings with each other
and with God. . . . When one of you says, "I'm on Paul's side," and
another says, "I'm for Apollos," aren't you being totally infantile?

Who do you think Paul is, anyway? Or Apollos, for that matter?
Servants, both of us. . . . We each carried out our servant assignment.
I planted the seed, Apollos watered the plants, but *God* made you grow.
(1 Corinthians 3:1, 4–6, MSG, italics in the original)

Comparisons, whether imposed by others or ourselves, create pressures
God never intended us to bear. Grace has a completely different view. Grace
says to the people in our lives, no matter what their race, political preference, or
position, "You are what you are by the grace of God. I accept you completely. I
thank God for who you are and what you are becoming." *Without* grace we
tend to see things on the surface.

The thing that we need most in order to deal with the divisive issue of racism is *grace*. One of Compassion International's leaders in Tampa, Jason Sowell, defines grace in light of this discussion as "a refinement of movement."[8] We
often use the word *grace* or *graceful* in referring to someone's manner or nature
or tone. We say "She is a graceful dancer" or "Their words toward us were full
of grace." So, the way a dancer moves on the floor or the way our words pour
from our mouths can represent certain "refinements of movement."

We really need such a refinement!

With Grace in Place

Grace-full moments. We can't live without them. When we extend grace to
others, despite our flaws and weaknesses, we reflect something of the very nature and character of Christ.

With grace, sin becomes the enemy, not people. What was it that enabled
Paul to endure such sinful opposition and rotten attitudes from a group of
people (the Corinthian church) for whom he risked his life to reach for Christ?

What was it that kept him coming back and writing, instructing, and teaching, even when it seemed that none of it was sinking in?

With grace, our souls enlarge and we give people space. What Paul wanted from the Corinthians had nothing to do with their graceless suspicions of him or his differences from them. His gracious heart and concern are easy to detect in a few of his last written words to them: "Now I am ready to visit you for the third time, and I will not be a burden to you, because what I want is not your possessions but you. . . . I will very gladly spend for you everything I have and expend myself as well. If I love you more, will you love me less?" (2 Corinthians 12:14–15).

The attitudes and issues facing the young church at Corinth would have drawn a scathing rebuke from many other leaders. Paul chose, however, to speak the truth in a spirit of love, because the Christ he had come to know was "full of *grace* and truth" (John 1:14). Accordingly, Paul reflected to them what he had already received from God. He gave them grace and he gave them space.

How refreshing it is to be in the company of a gracious person. Gracious people love without condition; despite our political preferences or doctrinal differences or ethnic diversities; regardless of our taste in music, clothes, movies, or hobbies; and beyond all our faults and weaknesses. Perhaps we are never more like God than when we give grace to someone.

So how can we, like Paul, become grace givers? Start by asking some questions:

- What am I living out of, grace or anger?
- What fuels most of my actions or reactions toward people?
  Racism or *grac*ism?
- What is behind the words I use as well as the inflections and
  tones in them?
- Do I believe for the best in people—or expect the worst?
- Do I expect too much of the people in my life?
- Do I look beyond the faults on the surface and see the desperate
  needs within?

- Do I endeavor to make people feel comfortable?
- Do I know how to give grace?
- Am I really interested in people who are different than I am, and if so, how do I show it?
- Am I more interested in others or just trying to get others interested in me?

We can get quickly caught up in the idea of a grace that makes a way for us to enter heaven, but there is another aspect to Christ's work on the cross, something he wants us to see today. Christ wants to use my life and yours to bring some of heaven to earth and into the lives of the people on this planet, in the real realms of our relationships . . . in the form of a gift called *grace*.

FEED THE FIRE
Questions to Ignite Growth and Change

1. How has race relations become such a big issue? Why haven't we been able to get rid of racism by now?
2. What role does grace play in dealing with the race issue?
3. What challenge does the race issue present to Latinos today?
4. What challenge does the race issue present to the church today?
5. What tools does the church have that best deal with racism?
6. Are Latinos in a good position to help heal the racial divide?
7. How can a more gracious Christianity help ease the race issue?

Answering the Prayer of Jesus

Drawing Circles of Honor

> What we need most in our world today is not just
> peace-keepers but peace*makers*. There is a difference.
> —Lacrae

When I (Robert) pastored a church in the Boston area, we were blessed to have around twenty different nationalities represented. But after a few years, I started to realize that while we had diversity in attendance, we were much too distant relationally. So we intentionally began to create small groups and events where we could share meals and get to know one another's stories. The results led to a much more unified and interconnected church.

At one of the connection events, we asked each person to write down on a card "one thing most people don't know about you." I will never forget the response of one Latina there. She simply wrote, "I am not shy." After hearing her share this, I came for the first time to realize that one of her deepest frustrations was that her broken and hesitant use of the English language caused some people to mistake her personality as a quiet one when in fact she had all the interpersonal strengths of an extrovert. Without our efforts at enriching community life, our view of this young wife and mother would have continued to be distorted and her experience with us frustrated.

Bowling Alone

When an early observer of the American experiment, the Frenchman Alexis de Tocqueville, toured the nation and wrote down his observations, he was intrigued with our rather unique sense of rugged individualism. However, he warned that if a strong sense of community and solidarity were not maintained, it would "inevitably lead to separation and division."[1] Many would argue that America is now experiencing major elements of this fracturing in our culture and in our cities.

Similarly, in his acclaimed research on community trends in America, Harvard professor Robert Putnam noted that there is a marked withdrawal from community life in the United States. For instance, bowling leagues have declined, as have much of our civic engagement, volunteerism, and social activities. Entertaining at home has declined 45 percent since the mid-1970s. Putnam attributes some of this to more mobility, career changes, relocations, and commuting.[2] Ironically, we have many more technological forms with which to connect to others, but there are many who are more interpersonally disconnected than ever.

A nation divided against itself cannot stand. History proves it. The Scripture confirms this. To be specific, it says, "If a kingdom is divided against itself, that kingdom cannot stand. If a house is divided against itself, that house cannot stand" (Mark 3:24–25). On June 16, 1858, Abraham Lincoln stood as a senate candidate on the floor of the Illinois State Capitol and gave a speech that would long be remembered. It revealed a soul conviction that would eventually prepare him for and propel him into a moment of unparalleled division in the United States. The most famous portion of the speech, derived from the passage in Mark's gospel, included these words:

> "A house divided against itself cannot stand." I believe this government
> cannot endure, permanently, half *slave* and half *free*. I do not expect
> the Union to be *dissolved*—I do not expect the house to *fall*—but I *do*

expect it will cease to be divided. It will become *all* one thing or *all* the other. Either the *opponents* of slavery, will arrest the further spread of it, and place it where the public mind shall rest in the belief that it is in the course of ultimate extinction; or its *advocates* will push it forward, till it shall become alike lawful in all the States, old as well as new—North as well as South.[3]

Lincoln saw that things in America could not go on for long in such a divided state as the nation found itself. In many ways, there are reasons to believe we are at a somewhat similar ethical crossroad in America. The difference is that the most awkward and controversial issue of today is no longer slavery but rather immigration.

Immigration and Conflict

In this current climate of debate and dissension regarding immigration in America, churches and church leaders stand at a crossroad. As raids continue, as deportations increase, and as cities continue to pass ordinances legitimating racial profiling, churches may be tempted to diminish or halt outreach to this targeted group in order to avoid the possible legal consequences. As a result, Latino immigrants may start avoiding churches—particularly those led by non-Hispanics. If so, major denominations such as the Assemblies of God, which in the last few years has experienced unprecedented growth because of its Hispanic congregations, may lose a significant portion of their membership.

Thus, almost every major Evangelical denomination, fellowship, or network has a stake in the Hispanic community. How pastors and leaders respond in this hour may determine whether Hispanics continue to forge strategic relationships with the non-Hispanic church or isolate themselves even more, confirming the old paradigm of Sunday morning as the most segregated time in America.

Although we can all agree that the United States needs to protect its borders from the entry of individuals who want to do us harm, the question pastors and church leaders must confront is what we do with the undocumented or illegal immigrants currently here while they are here. Up until now, the Evangelical churches in the United States have mostly stood silent on this issue. However, we Evangelicals have historically resonated with the conservative-driven tenets of law and order within our society.

Yet many white Evangelicals seem to adhere more to the rhetoric and philosophies of Rush Limbaugh, Sean Hannity, and Lou Dobbs than to the biblical guidance of Matthew, Mark, Luke, and John. At times, white Evangelicals seem to champion a warped convergence of nativism and spirituality, where being an American trumps our Christian identity. The fact is that while it may seem more simple and expedient to draw absolute cultural dividing lines between us, the realities of multiethnic demographic diversity and a Kingdom-of-God ethic make such decisions more nuanced amid critical tensions.

Biblical Directive

The issue of immigration demands that the church help reconcile this society founded on the Judeo-Christian value system, with the pillars of law and order and the promise of life, liberty, and the pursuit of happiness. Only the church can bring these three elements together, and pastors and churches must take the lead.

While political circles turn to various viewpoints often steeped in fear and biases of all sorts, where should Christians go to develop an ethic or approach to this deeply dividing issue? Does the Bible provide any guidance with respect to immigration? Biblical principles suggest a comprehensive solution rather than a simply convenient one. Leviticus 19:33–34 resounds: "When an alien lives with you in your land, do not mistreat him. The alien living with you must be treated as one of your native-born. Love him as yourself, for you were aliens in Egypt. I am the LORD your God."

Jesse Miranda, Global Chairman of the National Hispanic Christian Leadership Conference, sees the biblical mandate of reconciliation as pivotal to changing the debate: "For too long the extremists have hijacked the issue of immigration and made it a rallying cry for nativism and racism. We do have a legitimate immigration situation that requires our attention. However, the debate must convert to a dialogue, and reason must trump rhetoric. Racism is ultimately a spiritual problem, and it is only right the church become involved in seeking reconciliation."

In fact, reconciliation is the chief work of the church.

We cannot deny the fact that the immigration issue has potential either to further polarize our society or enrich our narrative. Hope embraces the latter. Hope that the Spirit of compassion, love, and tolerance stemming from a Judeo-Christian ethos embedded in our collective narrative will prevail and embrace righteousness and justice for all. Hope that the Christian community will rise up, speak vigorously from the pulpit about reconciliation to all corridors of our society, and demand an end to extreme ideologies from all sides.

Extreme attention is more needed than an extreme reaction.

Looking to the example of US history, whenever despair and desperation coalesced to threaten the defeat of reason, oracles of truth rose up to articulate the moral imperatives of practical, graceful deliberation. From the Revolutionary War, to the abolitionist movement, to the struggle for civil rights, our history has witnessed writers, scholars, and clergy making the case for truthful values compatible with a biblical worldview.

Is this a matter of grace or of truth? We believe Hispanic immigration will transform American Christianity by forging a platform of righteousness and justice, injecting the prophetic element of the Gospels, and activating a call to goodwill and love of neighbor. The great issue of immigration provides a great opportunity for the demonstration of Christlikeness, caring community, and wisdom. While many Christian denominations are in decline, Pentecostal-Evangelical movements such as the Assemblies of God are growing. However, it is important to pay close attention to the transformational specifics and changes related to that growth. A recent growth report from the AG notes the following dynamic changes:

- "Much of the numerical growth in the Assemblies of God in recent decades has been among ethnic minorities."
- "From 2004 to 2014, the number of AG adherents increased by 13.2%. During this period, the number of white adherents decreased by 1.9% and the number of non-white adherents increased by 43.2%."
- "The AG's growth in America is partly due to immigration."
- "About 1% of the world's population is AG. Fewer than 5% of AG adherents worldwide live in the U.S."
- "Pentecostal refugees who move to America . . . plant churches wherever they happen to land."[4]

So, the growth of churches in America "is partly due to immigration." Immigrants are helping to build the church in the United States. We believe they are also helping to build the economy in ways that may be overlooked by many.

The Hispanic immigrant Christian sensibility stands committed to a kingdom-culture DNA—multiethnic, multigenerational, biblical, and just. It declares the Kingdom of God is not red state or blue state, native or immigrant, conservative or liberal, Republican or Democrat, but is defined by righteousness, peace, and joy in the Holy Spirit.

Answering the Prayer of Jesus

One of the passions that I (Robert) feel most strongly is building authentic unity and community. My wife, Pamela, and I lead an organization called Teaming Life (www.teaminglife.com) that is committed to equipping churches, organizations, and families to do more than just "manage conflicts," but rather to also learn to "manage unity" within their communities or circles (a more joyous proposition). We do this through teaching, training, and consulting.

But at the heart of this effort is a passion to help answer the prayer of Jesus in John 17.

We ask so many things of God in prayer as believers, but what would it be like if we instead actually answered one of Jesus's prayers for a change? While the great cities of the world are becoming more and more diverse, more and more complex, the prayer that Jesus prayed to the Father seems even more clear and simple than ever: "that they may all be *one* . . . even as we are one" (John 17:21–22, ESV). His prayers were not for a particular platform or body politic but rather for the men and women transformed by the gospel into a family of faith.

Mark DeYmaz, the founder of Mosaix,[5] a ministry that equips multiethnic church development strategies, notes,

> It is significant to realize that Christ prayed we would be one for two
> very specific reasons, or "so that" two things will occur. The words
> *so that* in verses 21 and 23 are translated from the Greek word *hina.*
> This word, a preposition, is used linguistically to introduce what
> Greek scholars refer to as a "hina clause." In the Koine Greek of the
> New Testament, a hina clause introduces an "if-then" propositional
> truth. In essence, the proposition can be stated as follows: if X occurs
> (though there's no guarantee that it will), then Y is the guaranteed
> result. With this in mind, we can paraphrase John 17:20–23 to read,
> "I also want to pray for those who, in time, will come to believe in
> me through the witness of my disciples. . . . Yes, I pray that those
> who come after them will be completely united as one. There is
> no guarantee that they will be one, but if they will, there are two
> guaranteed results. First, men and women throughout the world
> will recognize that I am the Messiah. In addition, men and women
> throughout the world will recognize that you, Father, love them.
> They will respond to your love and receive eternal life through faith
> in me."[6]

But how do we grow toward being "completely united"? What are steps we can take in our lives, our families, our churches, and our cities to do so?

Drawing Circles

Building unity for us means learning to "draw circles of honor." Every person in the world needs a circle of honor in which to dwell, live, and thrive. You might say *we are never more like God than when we are drawing circles of honor.* The Bible commands us to do so ("Honor all people," 1 Peter 2:17, NKJV). When we honor the people around us and welcome them into the fellowship of that honor, regardless of the "differences" they have from us, we are answering Jesus's John 17 prayer and reflecting the Trinity itself. *As in heaven, so on earth!*

In a culture that's quick to *dis*honor, you refresh a soul by seeing a person the way God does, as someone created to reflect his image. When you draw a circle of honor around a person, you create a "sneak preview" of heaven and reflect something ultimately found in one place: the original circle of honor, the Trinity. Just by drawing a circle of honor, we help to answer a prayer of Jesus.

The fact is that the church today lacks the unity it needs to have. Too often Christians are divided spiritually and ethnically, while God wants a church that is unified. When people come together in unity, it is forceful, a formidable event, and heaven notices.

While a "universal unity" may be hard to ever imagine on this side of eternity and even something we would be a bit skeptical of anyhow, the unity Jesus specifically calls for is to be first and foremost among his followers, regardless of their background. The ethnic and political diversities of our world today provide the church with an unprecedented opportunity to display the "unity of the Spirit in the bond of peace" (Ephesians 4:3, ESV). We need to raise up many peacemakers. This challenge may also give us an opportunity to see the glory of God revealed in ways never before seen on this planet, ways that reflect and multiply many times over the unity displayed on the Day of Pentecost in the book of Acts.

A Forgotten Word

For me (Robert), the word *honor* has a classic ring to it. We don't use it much anymore, it seems. *Honor* evokes thoughts of kings, brave knights, damsels in distress, and chivalry. Or I associate honor with Asian cultures that generally show more respect for their elders and for one another than do Western cultures. The word also reminds me of the military, the Marines in particular with their famed "code of honor."

Certainly, honor still exists in some measure in certain pockets of our society, but for the most part it has gone AWOL, being poorly replaced instead with the cheap substitutes of self-actualization and self-talk.

In the Old Testament most occurrences of *honor* are some form of the Hebrew word *kabod,* which means "heavy" or "weighty." It is a word also translated as "glory." It suggests the magnitude or greatness of someone or something, especially the "glory" of God. In the New Testament, the Greek word for "honor" means "to value highly, to esteem, and to not take lightly."

The idea of honor in the Bible is also deeply relational. It reflects how people in a group, community, or society relate to God and to one another. It is the glue of true community. The Bible not only teaches the importance of honor; it gives us what could be referred to as the Ten Principles of Honor. A closer look at the Ten Commandments reveals that each one has to do with one of two things: honoring God and honoring our fellow man.

Honor Imparted

Jesus honored others everywhere he went. During his earthly ministry he constantly crowned people with honor, especially those who had been dishonored and disenfranchised by the world around them. Think of all the crowns he placed on unsuspecting heads, among them the woman at the well, the ten lepers, a bunch of fishermen, tax collectors, little children, and even a widow who barely had two pennies to rub together; to each of them he gave a crown of honor.

When Jesus left heaven and came to earth, he stepped beyond the Trinity's circle of honor and drew a new circle. This first circle of honor he formed included all those who followed him, especially his twelve disciples. He drew them into a tight fellowship of honor and community, only to send them out to draw other circles as well. On one occasion, Jesus prayed to the Father about these other circles he had drawn.

> I pray . . . that all of them may be one, Father, just as you are in me and I am in you. May they also be in us so that the world may believe that you have sent me. I have given them the glory [that is, honor] that you gave me, that they may be one as we are one: I in them and you in me. May they be brought to complete unity to let the world know that you sent me and have loved them even as you have loved me. (John 17:20–23)

There is dramatic tension as Jesus intercedes between two great "circles" in his life: the Trinity and the body of Christ. He says that he has given his followers the same "honor" God gave him. And he asks that they be brought into a relational unity that reflects the same one he experienced within the Trinity: "that they may be one as we are one: I in them and you in me" (verses 22–23).

Little Gestures

Start today. Start drawing circles. Seize the honorable moments. They are all around you and often especially among people who may be different from you. Begin looking for people in your world around whom to draw a circle of honor . . . in your family, your church, and your community. And as you do, here are a few things to remember.

It Takes at Least Three to Make a Circle

When you honor a person one on one, we call that encouragement. But when you honor someone in front of others, now that's more than mere encouragement; it's an event! There is a reason that Jesus said, "And when two or three of you are together because of me, you can be sure that I'll be there" (Matthew 18:20, MSG). An honor circle requires at least three people: (1) the person doing the honoring, (2) the one being honored, and (3) the person witnessing this event. Once you have that trio (or more), you have the makings of a potential circle of honor.

There Is a Difference Between Flattery and Honor

Flattery is when we merely say something we think people want to hear, often in order to get in return something that we want. It is usually manipulative and, at the very least, disingenuous. Honor, on the other hand, is sincere and authentic. It affirms the good in people and brings out the best in them. The Bible says, "Pay . . . honor to whom honor is *due*" (Romans 13:7, NRSV).

Be Quick to Pass the Praises on to Others

When you are affirmed or honored by others, it provides you with yet another opportunity to draw more circles of honor. And remember, passing the praises we receive on to others doesn't diminish our moment in the sun; it just reflects more of it around us and on others. "Let another praise you, and not your own mouth" (Proverbs 27:2, ESV). And if Jesus was quick to forward to his heavenly Father the praises he received, how much more should you and I do the same?

Ultimately, honor is something that flows from God himself. It is something glorious, the atmosphere of heaven. It is best seen at work among the three persons of the Trinity. And honor is a crown Jesus himself placed on our heads and in our hands . . . to place upon others'.

When you draw a circle of honor around someone, something powerful happens. In a culture quick to dishonor, you refresh a soul by seeing the person the way God does: as someone made to reflect his image. When you draw a circle of honor around someone, you create a "sneak preview" of heaven and reflect something ultimately found in one place, the original circle of honor, the Trinity.

FEED THE FIRE
Questions to Ignite Growth and Change

1. How significant is the issue of immigration today?
2. In what ways does the issue of immigration affect our future and unity as a nation?
3. Is the immigration issue at all similar to the slavery issue of years past? Explain.
4. Can we be a part of helping answer the prayer of Jesus in John 17 for unity in his church? What will it take from us? From you and me?
5. Have you ever had someone draw a circle of honor around you? Describe the experience.
6. In what ways have we become a culture of dishonor today?
7. How did Jesus communicate honor to the people he encountered?

PART THREE

Changing the World
with Passion

Open Your Life and Grow Your Soul

Beyond a Voting Bloc

How Latino Christians Will Change the World

> Latino power will drive the American economic
> engine in this century.
> —Juana Bordas, president of Mestiza
> Leadership International

The so-called Latino voting bloc is one of the hottest areas of interest for politicians and political parties today. Some are interested in it; others clamor for it. Both the Republican and Democratic parties in the United States are desperately and frequently seeking to secure the support of this "group." Many of these efforts make one major mistake, however, and that is to consider Latinos as just one bloc or group. The fact is there is much complexity to the diversities represented by Latino Americans. They are not monolithic, and their growing influence is multidimensional, multiracial, and multigenerational. And as they continue to grow and develop socioeconomically in the United States, they will take on even more diversities and complexities in their religious, economic, and political views and leanings.

We believe the greatest impact of the Latino Reformation will not be in the voting precincts but rather in neighborhoods, in our schools and communities, and in church communities and at their gatherings and prayer altars. While many look for a way to "move" Latinos as a Latino voting bloc or market segment in their direction, they miss something much more important: *Latino Christians want to do much more than merely "choose the next president"; they want to change the world.* For the Latino Reformation this begins with prayer, will be fueled by passion, and will be carried out by unusual collaborations, unprecedented opportunities, and bold initiatives. *It will be less about political science and more about passionate soulfulness.*

While a Latino currently leads the Catholic world, the Pentecostal-Charismatic movement is increasingly playing a leading role in the ever-growing Evangelical Church, and Latinos are leading the way in riding both of these waves of opportunity and influence. Pew Research noted several characteristics of the Latino electorate in the United States before the November 2016 election.[1]

- "Millennials make up 44% of Latino eligible voters and are the main driver of growth in the Latino electorate."
- "Among Latino registered voters who are 'absolutely certain' they will vote, one-in-five will be voting for the first time" in the 2016 election. "In 2016, 57% of Hispanic voters say they are dissatisfied with the way things are going in the country, up from 50% in 2012."
- "A slightly lower share of Latino registered voters say they are sure they will vote this year [2016] compared with four years ago." In 2012, 77 percent were certain, and in 2016, only 69 percent were.

Regardless of these trends, the Latino Evangelical voter bloc is increasingly a force to be reckoned with in the United States. Each year the Latino voice and their place at the political table is growing. Latina leader Juana Bordas notes that "in the 2012 presidential election, Latinos forged a new political landscape."[2] Latino voters increased to 10 percent of the electorate

Yet in the 2016 election, the Latino vote became more diverse. According to the *New York Times,* for instance, "Nearly one in three Latino voters in Florida cast their ballots for Trump." Also, "according to a CNN and Latino Decisions exit poll, his support among Cuban-American voters was even higher: 54 percent. 'Definitely there was a hidden, secret Latino vote,' Jorge

Ramos, the Univision news anchor, [said]. 'We're seeing a new divide within the Hispanic community.'"[3]

The question emerges: Do Hispanics separate their faith activism from their political activism? The answer for many is yes, they do. However Hispanic born-again Christians attempt to reconcile this, they try to make their political action an extension of their faith. Those who are not born again have no problem differentiating between their faith. That's why some Hispanics have no problem voting for a Democrat who is pro-abortion. They see them as two different platforms, with one having nothing to do with the other. But Hispanic Evangelicals do see abortion as a viable, legitimate issue. That is why the majority of Hispanic Evangelicals to date still vote for a conservative person. In the Romney-Obama election, it was a 50/50 split, even though Romney was a Mormon, which caused great angst among many voters.

The influence of Hispanics and of Latino Christians will have an ever-increasing impact on American politics for the next ten years. It is conceivable that Hispanics will determine the outcome of elections for at least the next twenty-five to thirty years. This could very well be seen through emerging leaders such as Marco Rubio and Ted Cruz on the Republican side and the Castro brothers on the Democratic side. Arguably, all of them will be influential players in the American political experience.

How Close to Politics?

While Latinos and, more specifically, Latino Christians continue to increase rapidly in number and influence, more questions emerge: Just how close should the church be to the government? And how connected should church leaders be to government leaders?

Latino scholar and elder Dr. Samuel Pagan says, "For the church to be the Church, it needs to be close enough to the government to know what's going on but also far away enough to speak prophetically."[4] While "faith remains important to Latino voters," according to Barna: Hispanics research, "they are skeptical of too much mixing of faith and politics." This is not only true among Hispanic Catholics but also Protestants.[5] Thus, talking about faith and politics is a more delicate matter among Hispanics than among non-Hispanics.

While many look at Latino Christians as a voting bloc, they may be better viewed as an emerging religious demographic. It's true that Latino Christians do represent the quintessential independent voting bloc, that they are not simply Republicans or Democrats. In fact, they register more as Independents than any other ethnicity or ethnic group. Latino Christians are independent and independent minded. This shows up in their faith and in their politics.

Change Is Gonna Come

As this political force grows, it is important to underline the fact that Latino Evangelicals are so much more than an emerging voting bloc. While this is important and significant, there are many other factors and influences emerging among and for this group that need to be considered. They are not only on the rapid political and faith upswing in the United States, they are changing the face and flavor of the United States and the world.

Latino Christians possess a unique set of historical and cultural characteristics that seem to be right for the time in which we live. This influence and impact did not develop overnight. It has been in the making for quite some time. In fact, it has grown up so subtly yet so suddenly that many could miss it. That is one of the reasons for this book.

A reasonable consideration of the statistics and demographics depicting the growth of Latino groups throughout the United States and globally makes it unmistakable that Latinos are bringing some sweeping changes to the world, not only to "their" world but also to "ours." To deny these facts is to deny reality. To study and understand them is to provide opportunities, the potential list of which is almost endless. Consider the following "change effects" that Latinos and Latino Christians are having on the world around us and quite possibly on your specific community.

Change Effect 1: A Collectivist Culture

The concept of "power" or "Latino power" is quite different than what Anglos are accustomed to in the United States. Traditionally in the United States, power is seen as something limited to a few key influencers and is used hierarchically. It is more about dominance and control, and it is restricted to the wishes of one leader or a few leaders. Latino power, quite differently, is a collective power, a community influence. It is more about *we* than *me*.

Hispanic cultures are generally much more collectivist in nature than European or Anglo cultures, which tend to be more about the individual. Collectivist cultures are community oriented. They are focused on how people can grow, work, worship, and develop—together. This is a major component and characteristic of Latino culture.[6]

For Anglos living in the United States, we are entrenched in an individualistic culture that focuses more on our sole interests, opinions, and needs. Thus, it is quite easy to overlook the stark contrast and nature of living in a collectivist culture, one that is focused more on solidarity than individual success.

There are many benefits and advantages to a collectivist culture. For one, it is more in line with the sense of unity and community in the early church described in Acts 2:42–47. Second, the authentic sense of community enjoyed by so many Hispanic families, churches, and groups appeals deeply to the need for community existent among Millennials today.

Ironically, oftentimes in predominantly white churches in America, "community" is limited to the pastor inviting you to turn around for one minute during the worship service and "greet your neighbor." While this is at least slightly introductory to community, it will in no way quench the deep thirst for relationship present today in either Latinos or Millennials, and especially those who are both: Latino Millennials.

Change Effect 2: A Values-Based Culture

A second change is that Latino Christians and Latinos overall may help bring us back to some of our most valued traditions in the United States. Latinos in general come from values-based cultures. For instance, a Barna: Hispanics study showed that "overall, 69 percent of Hispanic adults support the idea of teaching 'values found in the Bible' in public schools."[7] Hispanics not only place a high value on family; they also name it *the most significant* contribution Latinos make to society today. They even rank it ahead of their cultural heritage and their celebrated work ethic. From the study, consider these findings:[8]

- "Almost eight in 10 (78%) agree that family is the basic building block of a healthy community."
- "Seven in 10 (69%) agree that a child is better off if he or she has married parents."
- "Two-thirds (66%) agree with the 'traditional definition of marriage'—that it is between one man and one woman."
- "Six in 10 (60%) agree that sex should take place only in the context of marriage."

At a time when so many Christians seem desperate to establish or reestablish values in our culture, primarily through government or political efforts, Latinos continue to practice it amid the nucleus of all human relationships: the family unit. They know that if you can impact and affect the family for the good, it will ultimately in some way affect the community, the nation, and the world. For Christian Latinos, their highest hope for the world is not what kind of president they elect but what kinds of parents and children they will be.

Change Effect 3: An Economic Force

Not only is the Latino cultural and family influence striking and full of yet-to-be-fully-seen influence, the economic impact of this group is enormous. Juana Bordas notes, "Beyond its cultural influence, Latino power will drive the American economic engine in this century."[9] The Latino economy is undoubtedly growing rapidly. "Hispanic purchasing power in the United States is more than $1 trillion annually and growing at a rate three times that of the national average."[10]

A few years ago the *Atlantic* wrote a cover story on the role that some big lending agencies played in marketing unrealistic mortgages to Latinos by manipulating leaders in large Hispanic churches. While this behavior was exploitative and reprehensible, it also showed how much those bankers knew that the next untapped economic resource bloc in the United States is Hispanics.[11]

While no church or church leader should go after Latinos with financial motivations, it is also true that their economic strength and influence should not be ignored. As they continue to emerge and grow in strength financially, Latinos will become an increasing percentage of the financial support for church work, compassionate ministry, and world missions. Their financial resources as well as their spiritual resources await godly teaching, training, and leadership from wise ecclesial stewards.

Change Effect 4: A Growing Workforce

For many years, Hispanics have been viewed as hard workers. In many cases they have been stereotyped in some minds as "those Mexican migrant workers." First of all, this is certainly a large group of workers in the United States. Also, they are much depended upon, as studies have shown that many whites do not want to do the work that so many Hispanics are willing to do. In many communities tomorrow morning, Hispanics will be the first to show up to inquire about day work available in the fields of fruit and vegetable harvesting as well as temporary construction work. The Latino work ethic is a thing of legend. The wise observer of trends and culture today, however, will be careful not to restrict their understanding and expectations of Latinos to day work. No, Latinos are emerging in careers and influence in every sector of society and none more than the world of business.[12]

While the United States continues to dialogue about an effective plan for dealing with immigration violations and issues, noted business consultant Rainer Strack points to another looming issue. In a recent TED talk, he explained the coming "workforce crisis of 2030" in which an aging world will run into a shortage of laborers in numerous fields of work. Many may not recognize this issue.[13] However, according to the Pew Research Center, the largest and most youthful emerging workforce entrants in the United States this year will be Latinos.[14] "As of 2014, there are an estimated 55 million Hispanic people in the United States."[15] Millions, however, are stuck in immigration limbo due to the political stalemate in this nation.

One thing organizations should remember is that "while the average age among whites is 40, it is 27 among Latinos." In fact, "for every Anglo that dies, one is born; for every Latino that dies eight are born." Latinos are now the largest Millennial group.[16]

Demographers are predicting that without immigration, the declining US birthrate and the graying of the white population will result in a dearth of workers and a faltering economy. "There were 59 children and elderly people per 100 adults of working age in 2005. That will rise to 72 dependents per 100 adults of working age in 2050."[17]

Immigration and the growing number of Latinos will sustain the US economy, take care of the elderly, and educate our youth. Consider that between 2000 and 2050 "new immigrants and their descendants will account for 82% of population increase." Latinos will triple in number and "will account for 60% of the nation's population growth from 2005 to 2050."[18] Janet Murguía, who heads the National Council of La Raza, connects this to our economic future: "The growing Latino population ensures the steady supply of future workers and taxpayers needed to maintain the social contract between generations."[19]

After consideration of these statistics, we may find that Hispanic immigration in the United States is not just a problem to face. In some aspects, it may very well prove to be a blessing and a gift from God—even one that bolsters our economy.

Change Effect 5: A Place for Women to Emerge

Women will have a significant role in the future of the Latino church. In many places, the Latino culture is very matriarchal. As mentioned earlier, some say within the culture, "The man wears the pants in the family, but the woman tells him which pair to wear!" It should be noted that there is still some angst and familial turmoil in certain areas, more in the Mexican *machista* culture and in some South American settings, but less so in the Caribbean.

Not only are Latino workers rapidly emerging and full of potential for organizations of all kinds, but also churches, businesses, and other organizations developed by Latinos are providing many opportunities for women to emerge. This is not only true in the United States but also around the world.

I (Robert) see this powerfully at work in churches in Peru and other Latin American regions. It is becoming more and more common, for example, to see husband-wife pastoring teams in these settings. Not only that, in many cases husbands and wives share aspects of the leading and the preaching responsibilities with each other.

Pentecostals throughout the world, from Azusa Street on, have often cited the events of the Day of Pentecost (Acts 2:17) as a fulfillment of the prophecy of Joel:

> And it shall come to pass afterward,
>> that I will pour out my Spirit on all flesh;
> your sons and your daughters shall prophesy,
>> your old men shall dream dreams,
>> and your young men shall see visions. (Joel 2:28, ESV)

Considered in context, the most astounding aspect of this prophecy in its day was the phrase *"and your daughters."* The biggest revelation in the sense of a clarification in this word or promise from God was related to the bold involvement of women in the work of God and of his Spirit. God promised to pour out his Spirit not only on the men but also on the women. In context this was a countercultural, revolutionary promise. In fact, "women solo-pastor some of the most dynamic Latino churches."[20]

Change Effect 6: Uniquely Linked to the World

One of the greatest opportunities that Latinos possess today is related to their growing global interconnectedness. Church and business leaders alike are wise to keep in mind that when you connect with someone new you also have the potential opportunity of not only relating to them but also eventually connecting with several people who make up their network of family, friends, and associates. This is true with just about anyone you meet because of technology and social media. However, it is even truer with Latinos for one major reason: Latinos are vitally linked to the world village and are "the bridge linking North, South, and Central America." Hispanics are, in fact, connected to some twenty-six countries by virtue of their language, culture, and family.[21]

The Latinization of America

Not only are we experiencing the salsafication of the church, we are also experiencing to a great extent the Latinization of America. This, of course, does not mean that everyone is going to become Hispanic. Rather, it means that virtually everyone will feel the influence and impact of Latin life and culture in the United States.

Not only is the process of Latinization affecting the way people eat and feel, in some ways and places, it is changing the way they worship. For instance, at the university where I (Robert) teach in Florida, just one year ago our chapels were predominantly led by white pastors and musicians. In the last year alone, we have added a Latino campus pastor and a Latino worship leader as an assistant campus pastor. The percentage of Hispanics attending Southeastern University in recent years has increased from 13 percent in 2011 to 18 percent in 2016.

While many Hispanics in America have learned to speak English, many of the parents and grandparents insist that they use Spanish in their homes. This is to preserve a cherished part of their heritage and to help them not lose connections with their extended family members across the world.

Increasingly, however, the use of Spanish is present in American culture, both in church and at work. "The United States is quickly becoming a bilingual nation and just passed Spain as the country with the second-highest number of Spanish speakers."[22]

Change Effect 7: A Cultural Oasis: Acculturation Versus Assimilation

When European immigrants landed on Ellis Island, they were advised to change their names, lose their language, and "shed their cultural skin." They were urged to "assimilate" and never "look back." Since their cultural and religious backgrounds were so similar, they made this step collectively in the hopes of experiencing the American dream. The nation was young and still "forging its identity."[23]

As mentioned in chapter 8, Hispanics coming to America practiced more acculturation than assimilation. Instead of leaving their culture behind, they brought it with them—for a couple of reasons. One of them is the discrimination and racism they were subjected to; this kept them away. Another reason is the relatively easy access many of them have had to their Hispanic homelands via communication and travel.

The Skill of the Age: Cultural Intelligence

In the 1990s, Daniel Goleman made a compelling case for the importance of emotional intelligence or emotional quotient (EQ) in the lives of today's employers and employees. Similarly, we need to be truly informed about cultural matters.[24] *Cultural intelligence* or *cultural quotient* (CQ) is a term used in business, education, government, and academic research. Cultural intelligence can be understood as the capability to relate to and work effectively across cultures. One of the best ways to make someone feel cared for or loved is to simply listen to the person, to really hear what the person has to say and appreciate what the person feels. David Augsburger said, "Being heard is so close to being loved that for the average person, they are almost indistinguishable."

Dr. Samuel Pagan warns against approaching Latinos purely from a political view or for a political purpose. As a church leader, he notes that "politics are splitting the church on many fronts and the Hispanic church is no exception. Ministers need to be wise in how they use their pulpits when it comes to politics. Sociopolitically, churches want to impact their communities. But there is a growing lack of trust for political systems among Hispanics."[25]

While politicians may invest millions to "crack the code" to secure more of the "Latino voting bloc," the wisest among us will go beyond statistical analytics. Instead of crunching the numbers, they will inquire personally and with great interest. They won't just study spreadsheets; they will ask questions and study the souls of Latinos by seeking to get a glimpse of life through their lens.

Pagan predicts, "In the next ten years a movement is coming among Hispanics towards more-independent churches. There will be no more brand loyalty but more church shopping based on issues of convenience." He says that among Hispanics there will be three types of churches:

1. **New Generation Churches**—made up of recent arrivals or immigrants. These services will be conducted all in Spanish.
2. **Bilingual Congregations**—where the older people will speak Spanish, the younger ones English.
3. **All-English-Speaking Hispanic Churches**—such as Cornerstone Church in San Diego, pastored by Sergio de la Mora.[26]

Churches and church leaders have a rare opportunity today to get to know and love the Latinos in their communities. But instead of waiting to impersonally engage a "voting bloc," the much-better way is to more personally connect with men and women in your community. It starts with interest and caring enough to ask and inquire. It continues with a good meal together, conversation, and friendship.

FEED THE FIRE
Questions to Ignite Growth and Change

1. *Have some people underestimated the impact of Latino Evangelicals? Explain.*
2. *What is the danger of relegating Latino Evangelicals to a "voting bloc"?*
3. *What change effects do you believe Latinos will most contribute to in the future?*
4. *What opportunities do Latino Evangelicals have in front of them today?*
5. *How can churches of all kinds connect better with Latinos in their communities?*
6. *In what types of churches will Latinos in America feel most at home?*
7. *What steps can you and your church or organization take to better serve Latino Evangelicals?*

Next-Gen Latinos

How They Will Be Led

Latinos are stirring the salsa and gusto into leadership.
—Juana Bordas

Jesse Miranda is a catalytic leader who has been at the forefront of much of what is now the Latino Evangelical movement. The younger men in various roles of leadership in this movement affectionately know him as a spiritual father, if not "godfather." It would be difficult to overestimate the impact of his efforts, vision, and leadership on this dynamic and rapidly growing movement. Chief among his guiding values is his investment in the next generation of Latino leaders.

I (Samuel) view him as an "Elijah" in my life. He has passed a baton to me that I intend to, in turn, pass to the next generation. In addition to holding a doctor of ministry degree from Fuller Seminary, Miranda has taught at Vanguard University and lectured at many others. He also serves as an executive presbyter with the Assemblies of God and is the first Latino to ever serve on the national board as well as the first to ever speak at a General Council (1985). While accomplishing so much for the Kingdom of God and Latino Evangelicals, all the while he has kept his eye on the next generation.

Robert and I believe a key to effective church ministry today is not only a multiethnic strategy but a multigenerational one as well. For the first time in American history more minority babies are now being born each day than are those of the majority (or white babies). On July 1, 2015, the ratio of "racial or ethnic [minority]" babies was 50.2 percent.[1] This trend has existed for a while, as in the 2014–15 school year it was reported that for the first time more minority students than white students were enrolled in the United States.[2] The Census Bureau reports that "around the time the 2020 Census is conducted, more than half of the nation's children are expected to be part of a minority race or ethnic group."[3]

Pew Research also confirms several vital characteristics of Hispanic Millennials.[4]

- Latino Millennials "are the youngest major racial or ethnic group in the United States."
- "About one-third, or 17.9 million, of the nation's Hispanic population is younger than 18."
- "Nearly six-in-ten Hispanics are Millennials or younger," while "half of the black population," "46% of the . . . Asian population," and "only about four-in-ten" of whites "are Millennials or younger."
- In 2014, the median age of Latinos was twenty-eight, compared to thirty-three for blacks, thirty-six for Asians, and forty-three for whites.

In 2008, I (Samuel) wrote that "[The Latino] community's future growth capacity is dramatic: 75 percent of Hispanics are under 40 years of age. . . . By [2009], one out of every six Americans will be of Hispanic descent, and by 2020, the Latino population will total roughly 102.6 million people or 24 percent of the population."

A Barna: Hispanics report found that while 52 percent of Latino parents said that the local church is critical in their children's lives, only 21 percent said that "the church addresses youth challenges well." Additionally,

when it comes to the things that Hispanics believe have a strong impact on Hispanic youth, the most common perceived influence tends to be relationships, such as family (66%), peers (62%), and

educators (43%). Hispanics, like other adults, seem to under-
estimate the influence of media on youth, particularly "older"
media like television, movies, and music. Church programs (35%)
and the Bible (29%) are deemed to be the least influential elements
on today's young Hispanics.[5]

In early segments of this book, we discussed the fact that many Latinos are losing their youth from the church. This is a crisis that requires attention, prayer, and intentional efforts. Lost sheep need determined shepherds with hearts on fire for their salvation.

Bringing Changes

Next-Gen Latinos are also changing the church. I believe they are rejecting legalism and Pharisaic spiritual behavior (that is, "Watch how spiritual I am"). They are rejecting strong, rigorous, conservative, and one-dimensional approaches to life and faith. They are embracing churches and organizations that are more culturally relevant and more optically pleasing.

While Next-Gen Latino Christians are bringing changes, they still want biblical truth. But many of them want a "cool Christianity" (which may have some inherent issues of its own to consider). They also want to marry their Latino experience with American culture. They don't see it as an either-or proposition. While many of them are functioning as beautiful, passionate, and prophetic "Elishas" in their circles, they still know how to push the plow and serve. Also, they are committed to honoring the "Elijahs" in their churches and families, but they also want to see the contaminated waters of Jericho (see 2 Kings 2:19–22) healed in the name of Jesus. They want to be a part of a righteousness and justice movement.

Young Hispanics today are more ambitious than ever yet also face several challenges in achieving their life goals. A strong work ethic and extraordinary adaptability are key strengths that Latino Millennials bring to the workplace, church, and community. But this somewhat legendary ethic and the values upon which it is based did not come without a price. In fact, their ancestors sacrificed much to forge the determined and overcoming outlook held by many Latino millennials.[6]

Millennial Mind-set

The best way to experience the future demographics of America is to walk into an urban school and just observe. Juana Bordas notes that "forty percent of Millennials are already Black, Brown, Asian, and American Indian, and a growing percentage are beautiful mixed races."[7] Thom Rainer and his son, Jess, cowrote *The Millennials: Connecting to America's Largest Generation.* Jess notes that for Millennials, "Diversity has always been a part of my life. . . . Millennials have friends who look different, act different, and believe different. . . . We are diverse."[8] Millennials have a great propensity for embracing their own cultural traditions while appreciating those of others.

Millennial mind-sets are also fueled by a certain set of values. Among them is one that in essence says, "I want to live simply so others can simply live." Research shows that they want to live lives of purpose. Max Stier says, "The millennial generation is . . . more interested in making a difference than making a dollar."[9]

Latino Leadership in History

"Historical events have shaped the governmental institutions and practices for the countries in Latin America. . . . The shared experiences among people in a country produce expectations regarding governance that become passed through generations, not only driving the policies and social structures . . . but also affecting the cultural values and collective mental models."[10] They influence the soul or nature of leadership, leadership practices, and church and workplace environments in significant ways.

"Historically, in Latin America those who emerged to lead social change and transitional governments relied on autocratic, populist, and paternalistic leadership styles."[11] Several Latin America cultures steeped in traditions of machismo further underlined these values.

"Autocratic styles draw on positional power, paternalism promises some form of protection and care in exchange for loyalty, and populist styles are based on claims that the leader serves the interests of the masses (versus elites and power groups). Through the years, these styles have provided a strong framework for the type of leader who is perceived as effective in this region."[12]

In the world-renowned leadership-style study, the GLOBE Study, the highest score of all regional groups in the self- or group-protective category went to Latin America, a region characterized by solidarity and collectivism— not only familial but also vocational and ecclesiastical. While the Latin America region, however, has been more known over the years ecclesiastically for hierarchical models, trends show that emerging generations there will respond more readily in the future to organizational theories and practices more conducive to communitarian values and teamwork. Thus, there will likely be more of a move toward more organic models. The GLOBE research, in fact, reveals a high response potential to a team-oriented form of organization and organizational theory. The trend is accelerated among Latin Americans in the United States. Some Latino churches and organizations today are recognizing this trend already and moving toward new models of leadership, organization, and development.[13]

Questions Next-Gen Latinos Are Asking of Those Who Would Lead Them

Wise leaders today are taking steps to engage with Hispanic Millennials and helping them become leaders. One of the best ways to do so is to seek to understand and respond to the questions they are asking. Research shows the most common questions.

Question 1: Are Your Hopes for My Future as Bright as Mine?

One study, conducted by the National Council of La Raza (NCLR), found that Latino Millennials "have high career ambitions and value professional growth." So they are deeply desirous of "career opportunities that will allow them to gain experience and grow professionally." In fact, in one poll, "nearly two in three (65%) expressed concern about a lack of career advancement opportunities in the U.S."[14]

"Millennials are often stereotyped as having little attachment or allegiance to their employers." However, the research showed that Millennials expect a reciprocal relationship with employers. In other words, young workers want to become established in places that offer empowerment from leadership and "opportunities for growth" and development. Training, enrichment, and skill-development opportunities are also essential to retention of Hispanic workers.[15] In light of these insights, leaders, churches, and other organizations would be wise to provide clear pathways of growth and development for their personnel and volunteers.

For the church, we have a gift unlike any other to offer to Next-Gen Latinos. That is hope—*esperanza*. Of all the things young Latinos need from their leaders, it is a set of eyes that view them not just as they are but as they can be and will be by the grace of God. We need to see the "oaks of righteousness" inside the tiny sprigs of youth and take time to teach, preach, challenge, equip, and speak to their potential (Isaiah 61:3).

Question 2: Does Your Culture Have Room for Mine?

Cultural considerations are vital for church leaders and employers today. Not only should skills be considered; it is also important that culture be appreciated. Some organizations today have taken on the practice of "compensating employees for their bilingualism," in particular if it adds to the effectiveness and production of the organization. "Recognizing and rewarding the added value that Hispanics bring to the workplace" or other organizations will help in "attracting and retaining" them as well.[16]

Hispanic Millennials are proud of their culture. If you are an interested pastor, employer, or coworker, a Latino will probably like to show you pictures from his or her last trip to Mexico or Peru or to a sister's *quinceañera* (celebration of her fifteenth birthday) last weekend. Most Hispanics in America are bilingual, and three out of four speak Spanish at home.

One business-consulting firm noted from their market research that

Hispanic millennials have a strong connection to both their Hispanic and American cultures. They are predominantly bicultural and native born. However, keep in mind that two out of five Hispanic millennials were born outside the U.S. Hispanic millennials are able to choose the best of both worlds and will respond positively to brands that speak to their unique identity—*organically, creatively,* and *authentically.*[17]

One way of connecting with Hispanics at church or in the workplace is to ask questions. There is a list to consider at the end of this chapter.

It is also important to note that generational changes occurring today in churches, including the emergence now of third- and fourth-generation Latino Americans, make it important for pastors, churches, and Christian parents and grandparents to ask, "Does your church culture have room for me?" In other words, which do you value more: the preservation of tradition and culture, or the salvation of your sons and daughters? Numerous pastors are in the "valley of decision"[18] today and feel the need to bring some cultural and language "renovations" to their ministries. The challenge is to do so before it is too late. Churches that wisely and boldly make those necessary changes are riding a wave of evangelistic opportunity.

Question 3: What's in This for My Family?

Latinos are hungry to find churches that are family focused, that value the family and help them build and enrich their families' lives. Similar to the Aguayos and Salvemos a la Familia (mentioned in chapter 8), growing churches are finding ways to help build, enrich, and grow families. They are tending to the relational circles of family, church, and community. They are building circles of honor.

Latinos are known as being family oriented. Since this is true, they often work their jobs not just for their own provision but also for that of other family members and other generations, and in other countries. Many of them work hard to support the well-being of their siblings and parents, and in some cases their grandparents, aunts, uncles, and cousins. It is all about *la familia*. In light of this, many Hispanics face financial challenges unknown to their non-Hispanic Millennial friends and coworkers. Many Latino Millennials value the assurance of "family and career fulfillment" in their lives over the desire for "higher salaries." Options such as time off to be with their family members are highly valued.[19] One young Latina in the NCLR study explained her equation for happiness in terms of career and family stability:

> I want to be happy, and I think if family and finances are where you want them to be, then that brings happiness. We are only here for a certain number of years, and not everybody with wealth has happiness. So I think being happy is really important, and all those other things will fall into place.[20]

Question 4: Will You Lead Me with Humility or Just Authority?

Next-Gen Latinos don't want to be driven; they want to be led, led by leaders they can respect and look up to. Hierarchical or autocratic approaches are falling flat with emerging Latino generations today. While they certainly desire bold and prophetic leadership, they will increasingly respond less favorably to heavy-handed and manipulative leaders. We believe the kind of leaders they will respond to the best are teaming leaders, those who are more focused on empowering others than on being empowered themselves.[21]

In US culture, confidence and boldness are characteristics often highly valued. Employees are expected to be direct and full of self-confidence. This quality is often equated with capable, strong, and efficient leadership.

However, Latinos tend to value humility in their leaders. In some Latino cultures, overconfidence can be interpreted as directness, abrasiveness, and even arrogance. Rather, Latinos place a premium on humility among their leaders and the quality of maintaining harmony among the team. Thus, a humble manager with empathy toward employees may be viewed as more "successful" than the more seemingly self-assured manager and respected leader.[22]

Question 5: Will You Genuinely Appreciate and Value What I Do?

As mentioned earlier, in his popular TED talk, Rainer Strack describes what he calls a "workforce crisis" that will come by 2030.[23] He makes a case for the great need the United States and other nations will have for more immigrants to come in and help populate the workforce, as our current workforce grows to an average older age. Additionally, he cites the fact that from a "global survey among more than 200,000 job seekers from 189 countries . . . more than 60 percent" would "work abroad." He says that for "employees aged 21 to 30, this number is even higher."

The Strack survey also showed that when asked about their "job preferences," "out of a list of 26 topics, salary is only number eight."

- Number three on the list was "enjoying a great work-life balance."
- Number two was "having a great relationship with colleagues."
- "The top priority worldwide is being appreciated for your work."

Those surveyed wanted to know, most of all, "Do I get a thank you? Not only once a year with the annual bonus payment, but every day." People are looking for affirmation and recognition on their jobs.

The Church Will Lead Them

Samuel Pagan notes, "Millennials will represent a challenge for the established Hispanic churches." He cites that this will occur since they do not have the same view of "absolute values" held by their elders.[24] Their understanding of family and values is quite different. They are not as Word centered as they are feelings centered. Thus, the ethical core for a great majority has changed. This is a challenge the church must engage.

What a new generation of Latinos needs most is not a "new" Republican movement or a "new" Democratic movement, but rather a fresh Spirit-led Christian movement. Deep in their hearts they need to hear a prophetic call of loving God and reaching their world for the sake of Jesus Christ.

Millennials want something real, authentic. They can smell the fake stuff a mile away. They have a discerning DNA, the gift of discernment. They sense if people are authentic or not authentic. They are committed to breaking isolationist mind-sets. This means networking.

A Barna: Hispanics study cited the great need Hispanic parents have to "receive Biblical advice" and counsel. They are most interested in finding ways to help their children and teens "stay committed to church and faith during and after high school" (56 percent) and "make good choices in relationships and sexuality (56 percent)."[25]

Abraham-Isaac-Jacob-Joseph Links

In addition, successful churches and ministries must build a platform where Abraham's faith converges with Isaac's passion and Jacob's tenacity. In other words, leaders must implement strategies that connect the generations with a common purpose rather than focusing on the differences.

Craig Anderson, an elder of an Assembly of God congregation in California, fears we may be neglecting the older generation. "The music and sermons focus exclusively on topics for twenty- and thirty-year-olds, but what about the elderly in the church? Is there any way to address all three generations at one time?"

"This format of creating services for each generation was unheard of ten or twenty years ago," says Ramiro Quiroz, a next-generation specialist and denominational youth leader. "I don't see it as a negative but rather as a positive sign that the church is adopting business-model thinking and incorporating it within the framework of God's business." Furthermore, not only must we connect Abraham, Isaac, and Jacob via the presentation and delivery platforms of services and ministries offered at the local church, but we must also connect the generations via the avenue of a reconciled narrative. "Not only does there exist a generational disconnect but a biblical disconnect," explains Nick Garza, a doctoral candidate at Fuller Theological Seminary. "We connected the previous generations with the Word. The current deficiency in biblical literacy stands poised to impede viable transference of our Christian heritage."

Simply stated, if the Abrahams of our lifetime stood on the Word, and the Isaacs thrived on worship, then the Jacobs of our lifetime are crying out for justice. Can the church be a nexus of biblical orthodoxy, holiness, worship and justice? Can we stand on the Nicene Creed, worship in spirit and truth, and contextualize a narrative of justice?

At the end of the day, kingdom-culture Christians who stand on the pillars of generational connectivity will persistently cry out in the midst of moral relativism, terrorism, and despair to the God of Abraham, Isaac, and Jacob. Then the God who provided the ram, the wells, and the ladder will once again intervene for our generation and for generations to come.

Poised, Positioned, and Ready

A new generation of Latinos are positioned to have great impact on their communities, the nation, and the world. It is vital that older and established generations seek to understand and intentionally invest in their lives, their faith, and their God-given potential. Every Timothy needs a Paul, and every Paul, a Timothy. Titus teaches that the older are to train the younger and invest in their lives. Financial portfolios are not the only investments that matter as we get older; we have our lives, experiences, and faith to invest in an emerging generation.

Pastors committed to providing gathering places of worship that value the backgrounds and needs of Latinos will likely be the ones to win them and grow them. Perhaps the greatest need of the hour for an emerging generation is for seasoned men and women of faith to do more, much more, than focus on their retirement plans and financial portfolios. We have a generation to reach, to equip, and to launch into the purposes and plans of God. They are our greatest resource, and we must not fail them.

So to all seasoned men and women of God, we say, for the sake of the kingdom, make room in your circle for the next generation. Stand with them. Converse with them. Hear them. Challenge them. Encourage them. Believe in them. And make a place for them to serve and rise and, perhaps even one day, take your place.

FEED THE FIRE
Questions to Ignite Growth and Change

1. Have you experienced an older person investing in your life? Tell the story.
2. What did you think of the statistics about the growth of Next-Gen Latinos?
3. How will this growth impact our nation and the church?
4. What are some of the questions Next-Gen Latinos are asking of those who would lead them?
5. What can leaders do to better understand and serve the real needs and potential of Next-Gen Latinos?
6. How can the generational divide be overcome by the church? By you?
7. What younger person are you investing in? Is this a priority in your life and in your church or organization?

12

Project 133

As long as it is day, we must do the works of him who
sent me. Night is coming, when no one can work.
—John 9:4

I (Robert) could not pray the prayer he asked me to pray. After one week touring throughout the nation of Cuba and visiting several churches, I was asked to speak to a group of Christian leaders in that nation. Doing so was a privilege, but I was not expecting the request that came afterward.

"Would you do something for me?" the Cuban church leader requested. We had just met a little earlier in the day. I told him how after touring around Cuba and preaching in some of their churches, I was so blessed to see profound and visible evidence of God's blessing. These included: (1) a passion among the people for God and for prayer, (2) a commitment to meeting together often with other Christians for prayer and fellowship, and (3) an obvious involvement in supporting one another in spiritual and tangible ways.

After our conversation, the request for prayer came. "My brother," the Cuban pastoral leader asked, "I would like you to pray that the church in Cuba becomes more like the church in America. I see that you are prosperous there financially. Please pray that we become more like you."

My head dropped a bit and I said, somewhat reluctantly, "I am sorry, my dear brother, but I cannot pray that prayer. You see, I came here to teach, but after a week I find that I am more of a student. I am learning and growing from being here. No, I cannot pray that you become more like us, but I would like to pray that we become more like you."

The Test

The ultimate test of the Latino Reformation, as with any movement in the church, will be *how* it is carried out and what it produces in the hearts and lives of the people it touches. Will the leaders and participants in this rapidly growing movement remain humble, in tune with the Spirit of God, and attentive to following the "ways" of God? There is arguably a great grace upon the Latino church today, but "to whom much has been given, much will be required" (Luke 12:48, NRSV). With great opportunity comes great responsibility.

The temptation of any privilege, possession, or opportunity is the same as it has always been: to become prideful. However, as long as Latino Christians and those united with them remain humble and realize that this grace and blessing are not for hoarding but, rather, for sharing with the world, the blessings and opportunities will continue. While in this book we have considered many characteristics and influences of the Latino Reformation, what remains most important is serving the grand purposes of God and his kingdom. For this, we have to look no further than Psalm 133. The great question this passage answers is, "How would you like to be in a place where God not only *offers* his blessing to you, he *commands* it? What would that *require*?"

Psalm 133 paints a picture of something God and heaven find to be a glorious and irresistible sight. In a word, it is *unity*: "How good and pleasant it is when brothers dwell in unity! . . . For there the LORD has *commanded* the blessing, life forevermore" (133:1, 3, ESV). Unity is not the place where God *offers* his blessing; rather, it is the place where he *commands* it. The power and promise of Psalm 133 can be realized if we turn it into "Project 133" and apply our hearts to having a genuine unity of spirit. This can occur as we commit to drawing circles of honor in our family, our home churches, and our communities each and every day. As we do, the church, whether brown, black, or white, will be unified and God will be glorified!

The Rare Air of Unity

One of our favorite passages is Psalm 133. Of all the sections of Scripture focused on unity, this may be the most referenced. It is a goal passage or vision passage, something we should all pray and strive for. And it is best read with the end in mind.

Consider the final verse and promise of the passage: "For there the LORD has commanded the blessing" (verse 3, ESV). An important question emerges: How would you like to be in a place where God not only offers his blessing, he *commands* it? Now, would that not be a great place to be?

And just where does God command his blessing? And what place does he call the most "blessed" of all places? It is clear: the place of unity, where we dwell together in unity.

In today's divided world, unity is often a rare experience, a place that we too often miss or avoid or fail to achieve.

> Behold, how good and pleasant it is
>   when brothers dwell in unity!
> It is like the precious oil on the head,
>   running down on the beard,
> on the beard of Aaron,
>   running down on the collar of his robes!
> It is like the dew of Hermon,
>   which falls on the mountains of Zion!
> For there the LORD has commanded the
>   blessing,
>   life forevermore. (Psalm 133, ESV)

The Oil and the Dew

The writer of Psalm 133 paints the beauty of unity with two images: the "oil" (verse 2) shared between two brothers and the "dew" (verse 3) shared between two mountains.

While we work to overcome deep-seated differences, divisions, and prejudices among us, we must not forget that the twelve tribes of Israel dealt with many of these issues as well. After forming a nation under Moses's and then Joshua's leadership, they then waged war against one another, brother against brother, for centuries. This was the period described in the book of Judges. While Samuel and David reunited them for a season, after Solomon died, the tensions and divisions reemerged, and the rival kingdoms of Judah and Ephraim split and never reunited.

While Moses's brother, Aaron, no doubt caused him much grief and heartache through his compromises as a leader by forging a golden calf while Moses was on Mount Sinai, nonetheless Moses did appoint and anoint him as the high priest of the nation of Israel. Thus, this "oil" Moses poured over his brother was fragrant with grace as it ran down "on the beard" and "the collar of his robes!" Moses honored his brother. It was a rare moment—as is unity.

The grace Moses showed to Aaron is best expressed in how he responded once he found his brother had compromised himself so greatly as a leader:

> Then once again I fell prostrate before the LORD for forty days and forty nights; I ate no bread and drank no water, because of all the sin you had committed, doing what was evil in the LORD's sight and so provoking him to anger. I feared the anger and wrath of the LORD, for he was angry enough with you to destroy you. But again the LORD listened to me. And the LORD was angry enough with Aaron to destroy him, but at that time I prayed for Aaron too. (Deuteronomy 9:18–20)

David also shows that unity is like the "dew" that descended from Mount Hermon and covered Mount Zion. You see, while Mount Hermon rises nearly ten thousand feet above sea level, Mount Zion is barely twenty-five hundred feet high, hardly a "mountain." Thus, by size, Mount Hermon is the stronger of the two mountains. Similarly, Moses was the stronger of the two brothers, but he showed the magnanimity and the stoutness of soul to share life-giving strength and blessing with the "weaker" one. Unity comes about this way. Unity emerges from acts of humility.

The Future of the Movement

But unity is not uniformity. It is not just some static state of being but rather a powerful movement God is forming that is transforming a people to rise to places of service, opportunity, and identity. There are several components and characteristics of this work of grace occurring among Latino Christians in this season, and they will continue to powerfully emerge in the next few decades. The Bible says, "It is God who works in you both to will and to do for His good pleasure" (Philippians 2:13, NKJV).

While the following list certainly does not include everything God is doing or will do, it does represent some of the primary prophetic works we sense God is bringing forth from among his people today.

A John 17 Movement: A Multiethnic Church

This work of unity will arise and serve to better connect a currently fragmented church. We will begin by uniting the various branches of the Evangelical movement, and subsequently we will see greater kingdom collaboration between the Catholic Church and the Evangelical Church, particularly on issues of life, religious liberty, and strengthening the core institution of marriage across the world.

This work of the Spirit toward more unity in the church will include stronger Euro-American-Latino relations. Denominations will become much more multiethnic and racially diverse, or they will continue to diminish in size and influence.

However, these movements of Christian unity will not only build bridges among the races; they will also confront intra-Latino prejudices. This means that Latino Christians must not only work on building bridges to other ethnic groups but also do the same among intra-Latino relationships. While relational efforts are made between white, black, and Latino groups for the glory of God, it is vital that the same be done between Cubans and Mexicans, between Argentinians and Peruvians.

A passion for interracial unity!

A Billy Graham–MLK Movement

We described this in chapter 6 as the Lamb's Agenda movement. It is one that will unite righteousness with justice, sanctification with service, orthodoxy with orthopraxy, and John 3:16 with Matthew 25. A. B. Simpson saw this unity in a fiery vision of faith:

> The Holy Spirit kindles in the soul the fires of love, the flame that melts our selfishness, and pours out our being in tenderness, sacrifice and service. And the same fire of love is the fusing, uniting flame which makes Christians one, even as the volcanic tide that rolls down the mountain fuses into one current everything in its course.[1]

The future of the church is not salvation alone or justice alone. It is a fire-empowered fusion of both.

A passion for a justice-affirming salvation!

Greater Engagement with Culture

There will be more and more born-again, Bible-based, Christ-centered Latino believers involved in all major spheres of society. We will see more in media,

Hollywood movies, cable news, business, education, politics, government, sports, the arts—in all segments of society without exception. Not the least among these is the need to see Latinos rise in the soul-grounding and soul-deepening disciplines of theology and academic training.

A passion for learning!

The Gospel Priority

Not only will Latino Christians continue to grow and build, but it is vital that non-Christian Hispanics or those who are wandering spiritually in the community be winsomely introduced to the gospel.

A passion for the good news!

Putting the Kingdom Before Politics

While the people of God should engage government and politics, no church should ever allow itself to be defined by one particular political party or organization. A kingdom mind-set must trump all others.

A passion for kingdom values!

Winning Youth

Teenagers who grow up in the church and could otherwise become anesthetized to the gospel by overexposure to the mechanics of church must be intentionally and relationally engaged and evangelized. This will require older men and women to embrace the work of spiritual fathering and mothering in their latter seasons of life.

"The Latino AG is experiencing a greater number of second- and third-generation people leaving for non-AG Evangelical churches 'due to language, cultural, and generational specific deficiencies in ministerial outreach.' In order to counter this, [Sam] believes that the Latino AG must provide a viable integration platform that includes English language acquisition, educational resources, and family and marriage enrichment programs, or 'risk losing the next

generation of worshipers.' Preaching will not suffice . . . because these generations seek in their churches a vertical relationship with God and a horizontal
community of faith, where they can be encouraged to develop their God-given
gifts and talents to transform society for Jesus Christ. [Sam] argues that with
respect to Euro-American-Latino relations, the AG and its leadership must be
more intentionally multiethnic and racially diverse."[2] It is the cry,

> O God, do not forsake me,
> until I proclaim your might to another generation,
>   your power to all those to come.
>   (Psalm 71:18, ESV)

A passion for young souls!

Generational Linking

You will see an intentional multigenerational movement, one that brings together Abraham, Isaac, Jacob, and Joseph. This movement will bring churches
back to a multigenerational emphasis, meaning we will no longer see just one
generation worshiping in a church service. There will be intentionality in uniting the generations, where two or three or even four generations are worshiping
together on Sundays. Generational linkages must be intentionally strengthened, engaging every stage of life in the vital work of mentoring, modeling, and
effectively transferring power.

A passion for every generation!

Celebrating Tradition Without Traditionalism

It is important to hold on to the traditions of faith, culture, and family that
have bound us together over the years. However, while traditions should be
embraced, traditionalism must be avoided at all costs. While tradition is the
effective and meaningful transference of rituals and practices accompanied by

their meaning, traditionalism is the perfunctory practice of these rituals amid the loss of understanding of their intended purpose.

A passion for heritage!

Growing Leaders

Mature leaders must be developed: faith-filled men and women of integrity, grounded in their rich history and their attention riveted on their compelling vision for tomorrow. Jesse Miranda says that the church "needs to develop mature leadership that is full of faith, biblical and moral integrity, self-respect, and a sense of pride and history."[3]

A passion for impact!

A Wholly Healed, Healthy, Happy, and Humble Movement

This will be a well-structured, theologically sound movement that will engage people with the holiness of God (see 1 Peter 1:16), the healing virtue of Christ (see 1 Peter 2:24), healthy living (see 3 John 1:2), joyful living (see John 15:11), and humble living (see Luke 14:11; 18:14) where people emerge so blessed that they thrive and become a great blessing to everyone they know (see 2 Corinthians 9:8).

A passion for wholeness!

Moses: The Tri-Cultural Leader

Moses was not only a leader; in a real sense he was a tri-cultural leader. Interestingly enough, before releasing him into the role of deliverer for the Hebrew children enslaved in Egypt, God first allowed Moses to go through a series of sovereign circumstances to become absolutely immersed in not only Egyptian culture but also the highest form of it, in the very halls of Pharaoh's court and in the interest and care of his daughter. In a sense, before Moses came to live as a son of God, he was first allowed to live as a "son" of Pharaoh and of Egypt.

There were other factors that likely played a significant part in Moses's preparation and function as a leader. Remember, Moses's tumultuous journey toward becoming a leader of God's people took him from Egyptian culture to Midianite culture and into Hebrew enslavement culture. Consider these factors:[4]

- **Moses the Egyptian** was uniquely equipped to build a new nation. In fact, amid a community of slaves, he was likely unparalleled in his qualifications to lead. He was raised within the highest levels of leadership. He was a prince of Egypt and a government leader. He saw the ins and outs of systems, structures, and administrative duties. He certainly had access to the best education Egypt could offer. He observed international political relations and military functions.

- **Moses the Midianite** journeyed through challenging desert areas and entered Jethro's household, becoming experienced with navigating treacherous regions and a foreign culture. He successfully adapted from a palatial home in Egypt to a nomadic life, in home and workplace. He spent forty years serving in that life with sheep; now he would do so with people, the Hebrew nation.

- **Moses the Hebrew** had seen it all, from the slavery of his people to the halls of power and fame in Pharaoh's court. Yet he seemed unimpressed with power and authority. When God offered it to him, he did not grasp for it but rather seemed to shy away from it. Perhaps he had come to distrust what power could do to a man. He had seen power abuse people in many ways, and he had at least once fallen prey to that temptation himself.

The varied cultural influences and experiences of Moses had a preparatory efficacy on his development as a leader. The Mosaic model is one conveyed within the context of journey. The depths of the Exodus journey and struggle were such that they revealed the heights and depths of the grand themes of humanity, including advancement, conflict, division, struggle, hope, fear, promise, leadership, delegation, team building, scheming, dissent, war, antagonism, dilemma, law, rebellion, and many more. Thus the Mosaic model born in the developmental fires of Moses's tri-cultural tutelage has become the grand model for all human journeys.

The Church Jesus Dreams Of

We believe the church Jesus dreams of is a multiethnic one. How do we know this? Just read Revelation and the prophecy about the people of God in heaven standing together and worshiping:

> After this I looked and there before me was a great multitude that
> no one could count, from every nation, tribe, people and language,
> standing before the throne and in front of the Lamb. They were
> wearing white robes and were holding palm branches in their hands.
> And they cried out in a loud voice:
>> "Salvation belongs to our God,
>> who sits on the throne,
>> and to the Lamb." (Revelation 7:9–10)

We believe that wherever possible, every local congregation in America and around the world should be both multiethnic (not monochromatic) and multigenerational (not monogenerational). The Spirit of God brings unity and sets our faith on fire so that it shines for the world to see.

We believe in a multiethnic kingdom-culture presentation of the gospel that foreshadows our ultimate heavenly experience: "O what a foretaste of glory divine."[5]

Why settle for anything less?

FEED THE FIRE
Questions to Ignite Growth and Change

1. How did multiculturalism affect and change Moses as a leader? What role did it play in his development?
2. What is the challenge and promise of Psalm 133?
3. How could Psalm 133 become Project 133 in your church, organization, or community?
4. What aspects of the future of the Latino Evangelical movement interest or intrigue you?
5. Are there other emerging dynamics of the movement not mentioned in this chapter? Explain.
6. What would unity look like in your family, your church, and your community or organization?
7. Do you know anyone who is passionate about unity? How does the person live it out?

CONCLUSION

Enter the Joy!

You have been faithful over a little; I will set you over
much. Enter into the joy of your master.
—Matthew 25:23, ESV

It will take more than a sermon alone to lead the next generation. Young
Christ-followers desperately need the Word of God and a fresh allegiance to
the inspired truths it reveals, but they also need it conveyed in forms that extend beyond solely sermons, speeches, and soliloquies. They want to be led by
more than a sermon alone. Deep down, they long to be led with a song. This,
however, is not just any song but the new song inspired by surrendered souls
yielded to the Spirit of God.

Spend just one hour in a Latino Pentecostal church in Latin America, as
we both have on several occasions (especially Samuel, of course), and you will
know that if anything is present and felt powerfully, it is so often *joy*. Share a
meal with a group of Latino Christians, and while you will enjoy some incredible foods, you will taste the *joy* of rich community even more so. Since the "joy
of the LORD is [our] strength" (Nehemiah 8:10), this characteristic may be one
of the "secrets" of the explosive growth occurring amid the Latino Reformation
and churches today. It is a secret spice of salsafication, for sure. It is also something God wants to pour over and "season" his church with today.

Joyfulness is *salsafication at its best*. Interestingly enough, the Bible never *recommends* that we "rejoice"; however, it does *command* us to do so ("I will say it again: Rejoice!" [Philippians 4:4]). But we must remember that *joy is a choice* we must make, a discipline we practice, and a circle of community we share.

The fact is that one day our final destination will be not only entering into *heaven* . . . but, according to the Bible, entering into *joy*! "Well done, good and faithful servant; you were faithful over a few things, I will make you ruler over many things. *Enter into the joy of your lord*" (Matthew 25:21, NKJV). Salsafied Christianity is about entering into that joy every day! The joy of knowing Jesus and making him known! The Latino Reformation offers the global church today an opportunity for a fresh baptism of joy.

A prophetic moment reveals a song of joy that will celebrate opened seals, purchased souls, and shed blood. This song is not just for some, but for "every tribe and language and people and nation."

And they sang a new song, saying:

"You are worthy to take the scroll
    and to open its seals,
because you were slain,
    and with your blood you purchased men for God
    from every tribe and language and people and nation."
        (Revelation 5:9)

This revealed text exposes apocalyptic truth applicable today to the meta-narrative of redemption by grace. The elders and the living creatures sang a new song, and the song that shifted the atmosphere celebrated the Lamb's re-demptive work among people from everywhere.

There is a song that is the compelling song, the song of the Spirit, the song of transformation. Generations rising today need, desperately need, to hear the song of joy.

There is a song that can shift the atmosphere, a song that changes mourning into dancing, sorrow into joy, and water into wine.

There is a song that celebrates God's saving power among all people.

It's time for that new song! Can you tell? It's time.

"And they sang a new song"!

In order to sing the new song, we must recognize that the old one is fading out.

We have all heard the old song, haven't we? You know the "old song," the song of hatred, sin, racism, division, intolerance, fear, division, strife, and brokenness.

We've all heard the old song, and we are all tired of listening to it. The earth has grown weary of it.

Through the amplified surround sound of culture, media, and politics, our world stands inundated with the ear-shattering noise of an antiquated song that conjures fear and of mind-numbing melodies that inspire nothing but hopelessness.

We've all heard the old song, haven't we?

A dying generation sings louder than ever before the archaic song of moral relativism, cultural decadence, spiritual apathy, and ecclesiastical lukewarmness.

We know, for we've all heard the old song.

We hear the old song of terror in the Middle East, Africa, and even in America.

We hear the old song of violence amplified even in our own backyards and our city streets.

We hear the old song of epidemics and pandemics gripping our society with fear and consternation.

But praise God, we are not a people of the old song. We are the voices of the new, the new song.

In the midst of all the bad news, in the midst of the old song being played, we must gather today to sing the new song and, in the midst of a broken and hurting world, declare the truth: Jesus saves, Jesus delivers, Jesus heals, and Jesus is coming back again.

There is a new song arising! Can you hear it? It is deep within and longing to rise from a sacred place of silent hope to be a sound that will pierce the darkness. There is a new song arising!

This new song will *not* be sung exclusively by a black chorus, a white ensemble, a Latino band, or an Asian soloist. No! This new song will be sung by a multiethnic, multigenerational kingdom-culture choir washed in the blood of the Lamb.

But rest assured, this song rises not out of the programmed promptings of emotional exuberance but rather out of the depths, out of the leading of God's Spirit at work in the souls of surrendered men and women. It is not born of hype but rather of hope.

It is time to sing a new song!

The prophet saw it.

The Savior purchased it. This generation will sing it. Your generation and ours. Not just someday, but today. Not just somewhere, but here, here and now to aching ears so tired of the old song.

"In that day, everyone in the land of Judah will sing this song: Our city is strong! We are surrounded by the walls of God's salvation" (Isaiah 26:1, NLT).

The new song reminds us of our new identity.

As we sing, we know and remember who we are, then we can sing the new song!

So who are we?

We must respond with clarity, conviction, and courage and affirm the following:

- We are the light of the world (see Matthew 5:14).
- We are a city on a hill (see Matthew 5:14).
- We are people of the word (see Matthew 4:4).
- We are the salt of the earth (see Matthew 5:13).
- We are prophetic and not pathetic.

- We are disciples, witnesses, and Christ-followers (see Matthew 28:16–20).
- We are apostles, prophets, evangelists, pastors, and teachers (see Ephesians 4:11).
- We are children of the cross (see Romans 8:17), fruit of the empty tomb (see John 12:24), and products of the upper room (see Acts 2).
- We are the redeemed of the Lord (see Psalm 107:2).
- We are the sheep of his pasture (see Psalm 100:3).
- We are forgiven, free, and favored (see Galatians 5:1).
- We are called and chosen (see 1 Peter 2:9).
- We are warriors and worshipers (see Psalm 144:1).
- We are world changers and history makers (Mark 16:15).
- We are not Builders, Boomers, Busters, Millennials, or Home-landers. First and foremost, we are the church of Jesus Christ, and the gates of hell shall not, cannot, and will not prevail against us! (See Matthew 16:18.)
- We are not first and foremost brown, black, white, or yellow, Hispanic, Charismatic, Pentecostal, Reformed, or not. We are above all the born-again, blood-washed, Spirit-empowered children of the Living God!

That new song combines each voice in a chorus of unity. It's time to sing together.

If there's anything the devil fears, it's a united church.

While hell divides, heaven unites.

Jesus prayed,

I pray that they will all be one, just as you and I are one—as you are in me, Father, and I am in you. And may they be in us so that the world will believe you sent me.

I have given them the glory you gave me, so they may be one as we

are one. I am in them and you are in me. May they experience such
perfect unity that the world will know that you sent me and that you
love them as much as you love me. (John 17:21–23, NLT)

There is power in unity!

United, God's children entered the Promised Land!

United, the Israelites defeated the Midianites.

United, the Hebrew boys refused to bow and survived the fiery furnace.

United, the disciples prayed and waited, and the Holy Spirit filled the
upper room!

And they *sang a new song*!

The new song engages us with the chorus of prophetic articulation: *And
they sang a new song! They did not stay silent. They sang!*

Silence is not an option!

Silence is not an option when Christians stand persecuted around the
world.

Silence is not option when men abandon their roles as fathers, our children
are slaughtered in and out of the womb, pornography hijacks technology, God
is mocked, pushers are more admired than preachers, school grounds look like
battlegrounds, and our neighbors sit paralyzed by the "gate called Beautiful,"
begging for change (Acts 3:2).

Silence is not an option!

This nation will be saved when we desegregate Sunday morning, because
when we can worship together on Sunday morning, we can thrive together on
Monday afternoon.

In John14:6, Jesus said, "I am the way, the truth, and the life. No one can
come to the Father except through me" (NLT).

And truth, our brothers and sisters, must never be sacrificed on the altar of
political or cultural expediency.

The new song equips us with the outro of victory!

We will sing the new song of multiethnic kingdom-culture victory when we understand that there is no such thing as comfortable Christianity.

We will sing the new song when we understand that God does not call those who have it all; he chooses those who will surrender it all.

We will sing the new song when we preach the simple truth that the purpose of God is always greater than the brokenness of man. And that God does wonderful things with broken pieces! We will sing the new song when we understand that Christianity is less about promoting the perfect and more about blessing the broken.

We will sing the new song when we understand that Christianity is not measured by the level of rhetorical eloquence but rather by the constant flow of loving actions.

We will sing the new song when we understand that today's complacency is tomorrow's captivity.

We will sing the new song when we recognize that all people, in and out of the womb, carry the image of God—without exception.

So for the United States, for Latin America, for Europe, Africa, Australia, and Asia—for "every tribe and language and people and nation"—it's time for the new song!

So, sing, America, sing!

Sing, Peru, sing!

Sing, Ghana, sing!

Sing, all the nations of the earth, sing!

Sing, church, sing!

Sing, and walk like Enoch.

Sing, and believe like Abraham.

Sing, and dress like Joseph.

Sing, and stretch like Moses.

Sing, and shout like Joshua.

Sing, and fight like Deborah.

Sing, and dance like David.

Sing, and build like Nehemiah.

Sing, and pray like Daniel.

Sing, and pray like Anna.

Sing, live, and love like Jesus!

Sing to the Lamb these words out loud: "You are worthy . . . and with your blood you purchased men for God from every tribe and language and people and nation" (Revelation 5:9).

Sing a new song together with us, with your black, white, brown, yellow, and every-glorious-color-imaginable brothers and sisters, and let us change the world with a song, with *the* song!

Enter the song!

Enter the chorus!

Enter the multifaceted, multigenerational, multiethnic bride of Christ!

Enter the joy!

Racial Confessions
Black, White, and Brown

I believe that racial prejudice is mainly a result of one thing: Ignorance.

—Dr. Belle Wheelan, president of the Southern Association of Colleges and Schools Commission on Colleges

God wants to use the brown to help reconcile the black and the white. This is what we believe. We believe that God has raised up Latinos at this season in American culture to be, in part, a healing agent amid the racial divide.

Mark DeYmaz is a Latino pastor and the founder of Mosaix, a ministry devoted to raising up and nurturing multicultural churches, and he notes,

> I think Hispanics are in the absolute best position as a group to bridge cultural tensions and divides in America. There is so much history between whites and blacks that is not easily overcome. Hispanics have opportunity and are well positioned to do so. From a historical perspective and as a people group, they are not encumbered with the baggage that blacks and whites have between them. In broad brush-strokes, we are in the best position to bring understanding, unity, healing, and peace.[1]

But racial relations will not be improved without common ground and communication. Ultimately, our faith in God is a beginning place for a conversation, for any hope of understanding, to put us on a path toward reconciliation and healing. We hope in this simple essay to be at least a small part of that process.

Racism and Passion

Bishop Harry Jackson, an African American pastor and founder of the Reconciled Church Initiative, a movement committed to healing the racial divide in America, believes that ignorance weighs heavily in the ongoing racial tensions in America today. However, Jackson cites another factor: *apathy*.[2] *Apathy* is a word that is also associated with passion, but inside an ignited passion, it represents "a lack of interest, enthusiasm, concern, or passion." *Apathy* is *a-pathy* or "without passion"; in other words, the absence of passion. That passion is today in many ways a separation or separateness in living, the isolation that comes from a loss of interest in others, and particularly, in others who are different from you.

One of the challenges of the racism issue today, in America and in other parts of the world, is the enormity of the problem and its complex sources or roots. For some, the apathy arises from the feeling that racism is just too deeply ingrained, too long-standing, and too forceful to ever really cure or heal, a problem perhaps too big to tackle. So if we cannot fix it, why even get preoccupied with it?

Apathy is a dangerous approach for anyone to have toward the issue of racism, but it is extremely so for the Christian, for the person who according to the New Testament is called to the "ministry of reconciliation" (2 Corinthians 5:18). Instead of saying, "I could work with fellow citizens, schools, Christian schools, and other groups to educate or reeducate people and bring them to a higher level," we throw our hands up and say it is overwhelming and daunting. So since we cannot fully fix it, we won't do anything. For Christians, such a position is utterly unacceptable.

Additionally, the attitude that says disadvantaged folks in our community should just find some way to heal themselves is uninformed and unrealistic. That is not going to happen. The fact is that local churches and Christians are uniquely positioned to help solve some of these problems. If we really believe the problem of racism can be defeated and if we recognize that God is calling us to be one of the healing agents, it can happen. We are convinced.

A Spiritual Problem?

The question arises: is racial division in America today a spiritual problem? Yes, in many ways it is. It is a spiritual problem, and it has to be dealt with first of all as the heart issue it is. And yet, as Jackson notes, "The remedies, the steps to change are probably pragmatic, meaning closing the educational divide, bringing jobs to the hood, dealing with family intervention, so that families have an opportunity to come together, be healed. There are a lot of things we can do." Civic engagement is the responsibility of the faithful and concerned. People who feel they are beset by a lack of influence in the culture should engage the culture.

We believe one of the best steps churches can take is to become multiethnic. As this occurs, they could, in fact, address some of the issues in several collaborative ways.

Your Lens, My Lens

One of the biggest issues contributing to racial prejudice is the lens through which we see life. Whatever our racial background and experience, our view is affected and, at times, blurred and distorted by the disappointments, hurts, abuses, and neglect that have touched our lives and the lives of our family members, ancestors, fellow church members, and friends.

In recent months and years, we have seen a resurgence of protests and riots predominantly in many of our cities. Jackson notes that "one of the problems of anger is that riots and demonstrations often are an expression of the heart that says, 'I haven't been heard through the normal means, so now I am desperate and hopeless and I just want to get my voice out.'"

Each of us has a tendency to view racism and race differently, depending on several factors, including

- our heritage and experiences
- our friendships and relationships, or the lack thereof
- where we were raised or where we currently live
- our faith and the way it informs our sense of social responsibility

"I think the justice side of the equation is where a lot of blacks line up," says Jackson. "A lot of the problems with race that have hit the news recently have a direct correlation with social or biblical justice."

While pastoring in Fort Worth, J. Don George (a white pastor) realized he needed help to better reach and serve people of color in his community. He understood how to relate to white people but not to people of color, so he enrolled at the University of Texas to study black history and culture. Over the next few months, his world was filled with studying great leaders of history, including Frederick Douglass, George Washington Carver, Ralph Bunche, and Booker T. Washington. He also learned much more about Jesse Owens, Martin Luther King Jr., Thurgood Marshall, and Jackie Robinson. He says that during this time the "light began to come on in my understanding."[3]

After taking the time to seriously study and consider the perspective and experiences of African Americans, Pastor George experienced a paradigm shift in his view of the issue of racism. He describes what he learned about the differences that exist in the white and the black perspectives of the subject:

When we try to understand a different culture—on the other side of the world or on the other side of town—we need to determine what has supreme value to people. Some societies, such as WASPs (White, Anglo-Saxon Protestants) in America, view life through the lens of guilt and justice. To these people, statements are right and wrong, people are either righteous or evil, and the system of government should protect the innocent and punish the guilty. This description of cultural values seems entirely good and right to white people, but blacks see things very differently.[4]

Do you remember how people responded to the jury's verdict in O. J. Simpson's murder case? White people saw the jury's verdict of acquittal as a travesty of justice. The black community, in stark contrast, saw it as a vindication and validation of their entire culture. To many blacks, the issue wasn't guilt or innocence.

A guilty verdict would have brought shame on their race, and avoiding shame was the paramount virtue. Most whites value guilt and justice; most blacks value shame and honor—the two are sometimes worlds apart. What a difference it would make between the races in our nation and within churches if we showed more interest and concern in building bridges, such as people like Jackson and George do. Educating ourselves and asking one another questions would lead to more understanding, more unity, and more community. It would help answer the prayer of Jesus (see John 17) and certainly bring glory to God (see Psalm 133).

Honor and Justice

The understanding that Pastor George gained led to a deep change of perspective. He says, "When I began to understand the distinctions between shame-and-honor cultures and guilt-and-justice cultures, I saw that many statements and actions by white people are perceived as deeply offensive to the black community."[5] Once we understand this valuable insight, we don't have to change our personal views in order to relate cross culturally. However, we do need to acknowledge that, generally speaking, whites, blacks, and many Latinos look at life through different lenses. While some prioritize their deep passion for honor, others see justice as what matters most.

For years, George wanted to connect with and reach people of color, but it did not occur until he became intentional about better understanding them and their experiences. For him, this involved taking a university course. For others today, this may mean bringing a set of questions to the table and making more cross-cultural friendships.

"Whichever way we approach bridging the racial divide, it is vital that we face the problem and not deny or diminish its significance," Harry Jackson says. "And—especially in my conservation with white friends—they don't believe we have a big problem. They think that if people just respond to the status quo everything is going to be all right." The issue of racism is just not that simple. It is more intricate and ingrained in our society.

Considering the Other: The Challenge of Racial Afflictions

If we practice Paul's admonition to put other people's interests before our own (see Philippians 2:3–4), this will go a long way to helping us step out of our selfish considerations and look more fully through other people's lenses. When we take time to consider one another, to examine our viewpoints and the things that have shaped them, our hearts will begin to open more fully to one another. Some of the things we may find ourselves beginning to see are what we call "racial afflictions." These include a partial list of black pain, white entitlement, and brown precariousness.

Black Pain is something felt deep and long in the souls of African Americans. The roots of it stem all the way back to the origins of slavery, which was a foundational component of the early American economy. Although this issue was confronted somewhat by the efforts of Abraham Lincoln and by the Civil War, its insidious grip has wreaked havoc on the souls and sense of identity of blacks for generations. While some efforts have been made to level the playing field socially, economically, and educationally in America, a residue remains— one that runs so deep.

White Entitlement has naturally emerged in the United States. White entitlement, from their perspective, is the expectation that "since I am white, I can expect to have it better in life overall than people of color—a better life, a better job, and better opportunities." While few would make such a statement, many who would carefully consider their realties and upbringing would acknowledge that in some ways this has been their underlying perspective and expectation.

Brown Precariousness has formed from the awkward position many Hispanics have come to find themselves in. On the one hand, many of them have come to America with the same hopeful vision that has enticed immigrants to make the journey for three centuries: the hope of freedom, opportunity, and better lives for their families. On the other hand, however, now they hear much rhetoric that conveys they are not wanted here or may be taking someone else's job away. As a result, many Hispanics find themselves wanting to be in a place where they ironically can feel displaced and unwanted. Thus, they are in a precarious place.

The Problem's Contributing Factors

Some of the major factors, of course, that contribute to racism today include
- historical realities
- class distinctions
- a lack of access to education
- a lack of training and modeling
- generational poverty

Jackson says, "I would say class distinctions or lack of access to education are among the major factors contributing to racism." He thinks that due to generational poverty, people's horizons are limited, which frustrates and complicates the race issue. Many blacks and Hispanics today, for instance, feel they cannot make a difference because of a lack of education.

For average blacks in prison today, they have an educational gap, they are working below grade level, or they are functionally illiterate (80 percent of prisoners are). If you think about the lack of jobs, there are several other factors contributing to this problem.

From a Tower to an Upper Room

From the biblical record, ethnic diversities originated in the mind of God at first. It was connected to a change he brought about due to an organizational pride that formed among those who proposed to build a tower to reach the heavens. This is a metaphor of people trying to save themselves instead of depending upon God. As a result of Babel, today we have racial diversity. In Genesis 11 we find that at the tower of Babel, God confused the languages of the nations because, as Jackson notes, "a false unity was entered into and the aftermath of scattering at Babel that people wound up having geographic, linguistic, and racial divisions."

The Day of Pentecost, however, beautifully reversed the sin and resultant confusions of the tower of Babel. As God's people were gathered in the upper room to worship, the Holy Spirit blew among them like a wind and lit them up with a deep-seated, God-given passion (that is, "tongues as of fire . . . rested on each one of them," Acts 2:3, ESV). Their faith caught fire. Instead of the languages being confused and divided, they began to speak in the language of the Spirit. The work of the Spirit brought a uniting of the races. The Spirit desires to do that same work today.

Now, as a result of the work of the Holy Spirit, instead of being primarily referred to as many races or nations, the Word of God says that we are "a royal priesthood, a holy nation . . . called . . . out of darkness into his marvelous light" (1 Peter 2:9, ESV). Now, according to Paul, "There is no longer Jew or Gentile, slave or free, male and female. For you are all one in Christ Jesus" (Galatians 3:28, NLT).

Confession and Apology?

We live in an age in which the tensions of racism have resurfaced significantly, some of them stirred up by acts of police brutality and political disagreements. This has reignited scenes and sounds of protesting, boycotts, riots, incendiary rhetoric, debate, and cultural critique. Many of these acts originate from a desperate need to be heard and understood. However, there is another biblical healing practice that must not be left out of the equality equation, and that is confession and repentance. While many who are disturbed by racism and prejudice may only practice critique, protest, and accusation, it is vital that while examining one another's souls, we make sure we consider our own.

In 1994, an event occurred in the South referred to ever since as the "Memphis Miracle." At it, the Pentecostal Fellowship of North America (PFNA), generally an all-white organization, held a national conference in Memphis, Tennessee, for one major reason: to repent of its history of racial exclusivity. Black and white leaders came together to disassemble their former identities and forge a new interracial ministry. The climax of this gathering was a time when black and white pastors tearfully washed one another's feet while confessing their own sins and separations. Following a prophetic word delivered by Jack Hayford, the founding pastor of the Church on the Way in Van Nuys, California, a season of confession, repentance, weeping, and healing emerged. *Christianity Today* named it as one of the top news items of the year.

Bishop Jackson suggests that African Americans owe Hispanics an apology. He says,

> I think that African Americans should apologize to Hispanics and
> ask them to forgive us for our lack of compassion, because all of the
> problems we have at the root level are very similar to the class struggles
> and generational poverty of Hispanics (with some minor exceptions).

You have the Cubans in Florida that may be more well to do. But, by and large, we have the same gaps and challenges.

Right now there is something of a competition politically about who will have the biggest impact in election cycles. We are going to have to learn that each has its space and opportunities. I think blacks should have some confession that we have not included all of the poor in our struggles. There has been very little attempt to join arms in this generation with our Spanish brothers and sisters. I do think, however, that Martin Luther King Jr. expressed more connectivity with Mexican struggles in California.

In truth, it would do all parties in the racial divide good to consider what they might express or confess. We desperately need to communicate both truth and grace so that we might come to a place of reconciliation and healing. While many groups consider what they must do to bring healing in their homes, neighborhoods, communities, and country, our prayer and hope is that in your circles of relationship and community, you will begin and continue to do so and will urge others to do the same.

The Church: Modeling Unity

Latino Christ-followers are in a position to model unity as forerunners for the rest of the body of Christ and then the church for the rest of the nation. There are a number of ways that racial reconciliation can be attempted, developed, and achieved.

Growing Multiethnic Church Cultures. Predominantly white churches established in cities and communities that are becoming more ethnically diverse must intentionally develop the cultural intelligence needed to love, befriend, and reach the nations that are moving into their neighborhoods.

A passion for community!

Interracial Dialog. A lot of people think that just talking won't change anything, but talking is necessary to lead to empathy and compassionate strategies. In order to plan and work together, we must dialog.

A passion for understanding!

Reconciliation Events. One of the bridges of peace is having reconciliation events. For instance, one white pastor who runs a Christian high school in Texas decided to make discounted tuition available to people coming from black or Hispanic elementary schools in the region. In working on transportation or discounts, he created a feeder opportunity for some of the brightest of the bright who otherwise would be limited by generational poverty. So they are trained in a private-school, character-driven environment.

A passion for celebration!

Don't Say You Are "Color Blind" but Rather "Color Fascinated." All Christians must drop the quaint but uninformed notion of being ethnically color blind and instead seek to be color intrigued and interested. A denial of differences will not forge an authentic healing or union.

A passion for variety!

Drawing Circles of Honor. Every Christian must practice the much-needed art of drawing circles of honor in their communities and neighborhoods. The most-needed expressions of agape and honoring are not those that will be organized by church staff members and denominations but those that organically and spontaneously emerge in the most common places and in the most unexpected moments. "The LORD thy God in the midst of thee is mighty" (Zephaniah 3:17, KJV). "Make the most of every opportunity" (Colossians 4:5). Answer the prayer of Jesus: "that they may be one even as we are one" (John 17:22, ESV).

A passion for honor!

ACKNOWLEDGMENTS

We wish to thank

- our Lord and Savior, Jesus, for all he has forgiven us of and called us to
- our wives, Eva and Pamela, for the privilege of partnering in life, love, grace, and kingdom endeavors
- our children and grandchildren
- our mentors, Dr. Jesse Miranda and Dr. Robert E. Cooley
- our advisors and encouragers on this project: Rev. Guillermo and Milagros Aguayo, Dr. Juana Bordas, Dr. Carlos Campos, Joel Ceballo, Lissette Correa, Dr. Paul Corrigan, Dr. Harvey Cox, Blythe Daniel, Dr. Alberto Delgado, Dr. Murray Dempster, Dr. Mark DeYmaz, Dr. Alan Ehler, Dr. Kent Ingle, Dr. Harry Jackson, Russell Johnson, Gabe Lyons, Andy MacIntire, Shannon Marven, Dr. Daniel McNaughton, Rev. Sammy Ortiz, Dr. Samuel Pagan, Dr. Albert Reyes, Rev. Juan Rivera, Rev. James Robison, Rev. Samuel Santana, Rev. Tony Suarez, Dr. Zach Tackett, Rev. J. J. Vasquez, and Randy and Becky Young
- Albert W. Hickman, the senior research associate at the Center for the Study of Global Christianity at Gordon-Conwell Theological Seminary for his assistance with research and statistical information on the growth of Christianity among Hispanics around the world
- our publishing team: editor Bruce Nygren and the WaterBrook team
- the organizations we are privileged to serve: the National Hispanic Christian Leadership Conference and Southeastern University

NOTES

Grateful acknowledgment is made for the use of material in general from Barna Group and specifically Barna: Hispanics, "Hispanic America: Faith, Values and Priorities," published by Barna: Hispanic, a division of Barna Group, and commissioned by American Bible Society, National Hispanic Christian Leadership Conererence and OneHope, Barna Group, 2012.

Portions of chapter 4 appeared in a slightly different version in Robert Crosby, "Pentecostal Paradox: As the Global Chorus Grows, American Tongues Fall Silent," *Patheos* (blog), January 27, 2012; Robert Crosby, "Q&A with Samuel Rodriguez: Trends in Pentecostalism," Evangelical Channel, *Patheos* (blog), January 27, 2012; and Robert Crosby, "Rick Warren's Surprising Advice to Pentecostal Churches," *Patheos* (blog), November 8, 2011.

Portions of chapters 6, 9, and 11 appeared in a slightly different version in Samuel Rodriguez, "The Latino Transformation of American Evangelicalism," (Yale University) *Reflections,* Fall 2008.

The portion "Abraham-Isaac-Jacob-Joseph Links" in chapter 11 appeared in a slightly different version in Sam Rodriguez, "Transgenerational Christianity," Ministry Today, April 30, 2008.

The following people were interviewed by the authors for the aforementioned blogs, and their quotes are used by permission: Craig Anderson, Jack Hayford, Harry Jackson, Chad Lashley, Ramiro Quiroz, Russell Spittler, Billy Wilson.

Introduction: Those Salsafied Christians!
The chapter epigraph is taken from Dr. Luis E. Lugo, in Samuel Rodriguez, "The Holy Spirit, Hispanics, and the Transformation of the American Church (Pt. 1)," *Christian Post,* November 11, 2013, http://ww2.christianpost.com/news

/the-holy-spirit-hispanics-and-the-transformation-of-the-american-church-pt-1
-108478.

1. Karina Ioffee, "Boom in Latino Evangelical Churches Underscores Growing Population," *Mercury News,* August 12, 2016, www.mercury news.com/2015/03/23/boom-in-latino-evangelical-churches-underscores -growing-population.

2. Elizabeth Dias, "The Rise of Evangélicos," *Time,* April 4, 2013, http://nation.time.com/2013/04/04/the-rise-of-evangelicos.

3. Deann Alford, "Inaugural Invitation," *PE News,* January 12, 2017, http://penews.org/news/inaugural-invitation.

4. "New Census Bureau Report Analyzes U.S. Population Projections," United States Census Bureau, release no. CB15-TPS.16, March 3, 2015, www.census.gov/newsroom/press-releases/2015/cb15-tps16.html.

5. Sandra L. Colby and Jennifer M. Ortman, "Projections of the Size and Composition of the U.S. Population: 2014 to 2060," report no. P25-1143 (Washington, DC: United States Census Bureau, 2015), 1, www.census.gov/content/dam/Census/library/publications/2015/demo /p25-1143.pdf.

6. Dr. Samuel Pagan, interview by Robert Crosby, September 6, 2016, Orlando, FL. Used by permission.

7. Ana Gonzalez-Barrera and Mark Hugo Lopez, "Is Being Hispanic a Matter of Race, Ethnicity or Both?" Fact Tank, Pew Research Center, June 15, 2015, www.pewresearch.org/fact-tank/2015/06/15/is-being -hispanic-a-matter-of-race-ethnicity-or-both.

8. Juana Bordas, *The Power of Latino Leadership: Culture, Inclusion, and Contribution* (San Francisco: Berrett-Koehler, 2013), ix.

9. Gonzalez-Barrera and Lopez, "Is Being Hispanic a Matter of Race, Ethnicity or Both?"

10. Gastón Espinosa, *Latino Pentecostals in America: Faith and Politics in Action* (Cambridge, MA: Harvard University Press, 2014), 10–11.

11. Paul Taylor, Mark Hugo Lopez, Jessica Martínez, and Gabriel Velasco, "When Labels Don't Fit: Hispanics and Their Views of Identity," Pew Research Center, April 4, 2012, 1, www.pewhispanic.org/2012/04/04 /when-labels-dont-fit-hispanics-and-their-views-of-identity.

12. Bordas, *Power of Latino Leadership,* xvi.

Chapter 1: A Soul Moment

The chapter epigraph is taken from Elizabeth Dias, "Evangélicos!," *Time,* April 15, 2013, 2, http://content.time.com/time/subscriber/article/0,33009, 2140207-2,00.html.

1. "A Gang Member's Path to the Pulpit," Christian Broadcasting Network, video, 3:39, http://www1.cbn.com/content/gang-members-path-pulpit.

2. Peter F. Drucker, *Post-Capitalist Society* (New York: HarperCollins, 1994), 1.

3. "FFF: Hispanic Heritage Month 2015," United States Census Bureau, release no. CB15-FF.18, September 14, 2015, www.census.gov/newsroom /facts-for-features/2015/cb15-ff18.html.

4. "FFF: Hispanic Heritage Month 2015."

5. Paul Bedard, "Pew: 57M Hispanics Now in U.S., 17% of Population, 54% of Total Growth," *Washington Examiner,* September 9, 2016, www.washingtonexaminer.com/pew-57m-hispanics-now-in-u.s.-17-of -population-54-of-total-growth/article/2601396.

6. Bedard, "Pew: 57M Hispanics Now in U.S."

7. Juana Bordas, *The Power of Latino Leadership: Culture, Inclusion, and Contribution* (San Francisco: Berrett-Koehler, 2013), ix.

8. Bordas, *Power of Latino Leadership,* ix.

9. Wes Granberg-Michaelson, "Think Christianity Is Dying? No, Christianity Is Shifting Dramatically," *Washington Post,* May 20, 2015, www .washingtonpost.com/news/acts-of-faith/wp/2015/05/20/think -christianity-is-dying-no-christianity-is-shifting-dramatically.

10. Granberg-Michaelson, "Think Christianity Is Dying?"

11. David Masci, "Why Has Pentecostalism Grown So Dramatically in Latin America?," Pew Research Center, November 14, 2014, www .pewresearch.org/fact-tank/2014/11/14/why-has-pentecostalism-grown -so-dramatically-in-latin-america.

12. Granberg-Michaelson, "Think Christianity Is Dying?"

13. Paul Ames and Alvaro Padilla, "Pentecostal Mayor Prepares to Take Over Rio de Janeiro" *Washington Times,* December 1, 2016, www .washingtontimes.com/news/2016/dec/1/marcelo-crivella-prepares-to -take-over-as-rio-de-j.

14. Granberg-Michaelson, "Think Christianity Is Dying?"

15. Granberg-Michaelson, "Think Christianity Is Dying?"

16. "Christianity in Its Global Context," Center for the Study of Global Christianity, Gordon-Conwell Theological Seminary, June 2013, 7, www.gordonconwell.edu/ockenga/research/documents/Christianityin itsGlobalContext.pdf.

17. "Christianity in Its Global Context," 54.

18. "Christianity in Its Global Context," 54.

19. "Christianity in Its Global Context," 54.

20. "Millennials in Adulthood," Social and Demographic Trends, Pew Research Center, March 7, 2014, www.pewsocialtrends.org/2014/03/07 /millennials-in-adulthood.

21. "The Global Catholic Population," Religion and Public Life, Pew Research Center, February 13, 2013, www.pewforum.org/2013/02/13 /the-global-catholic-population.

22. Elizabeth Dias, "Why the Election of Pope Francis Is Important for Latin America," *Time,* March 13, 2013, http://world.time.com/2013 /03/13/why-the-election-of-pope-francis-is-important-for-latin-america.

23. Dias, "Election of Pope Francis."

24. Alberto Delgado, panel discussion with Robert Crosby, NHCLC Latino Leaders Conference, Anaheim, CA, May 2016.

25. Dr. Albert Reyes, panel discussion with Robert Crosby, NHCLC Latino Leaders Conference, Anaheim, CA, May 2016.

26. Dr. Samuel Pagan, panel discussion with Robert Crosby, NHCLC Latino Leaders Conference, Anaheim, CA, May 2016.

27. Dias, "Evangélicos!," 3, http://content.time.com/time/subscriber/article /0,33009,2140207-3,00.html.

28. A. W. Tozer, *The Pursuit of God* (Abbotsford, WI: Aneko, 2015), ix–x.

29. Elizabeth Dias, "The Latino Reformation," *Time,* April 15, 2013, front cover, http://content.time.com/time/covers/0,16641,201304 15,00.html.

30. Karina Ioffee, "Boom in Latino Evangelical Churches Underscores Growing Population," *Mercury News,* August 12, 2016, www.mercury news.com/2015/03/23/boom-in-latino-evangelical-churches-underscores -growing-population.

31. Ioffee, "Boom in Latino Evangelical Churches."

32. Sergio de la Mora, "Sergio de la Mora: The Pastor the Community Needs," *Outreach,* March 13, 2014, www.outreachmagazine.com /interviews/5425-being-the-pastor-the-community-needs.html.

33. de la Mora, "The Pastor the Community Needs," 1–2, www.outreach magazine.com/interviews/5425-being-the-pastor-the-community-needs .html and www.outreachmagazine.com/interviews/5425-being-the -pastor-the-community-needs.html/2.

34. David T. Olson, *The American Church in Crisis: Groundbreaking Research Based on a National Database of over 200,000 Churches* (Grand Rapids, MI: Zondervan, 2008), 16.

35. Olson, *American Church in Crisis,* 169–71.

Chapter 2: The Salsafication of the Church

The chapter epigraph is taken from Elizabeth Dias, "Evangélicos!," *Time,* April 15, 2013, 2, http://content.time.com/time/subscriber/article/0,33009 ,2140207-2,00.html.

1. J. Don George, *Against the Wind: Creating a Church of Diversity Through Authentic Love,* Kindle edition (Springfield, MO: My Healthy Church, 2012), introduction.

2. Jerry McCamey, quoted in George, *Against the Wind,* introduction.

3. George, *Against the Wind,* introduction.

4. Dr. Albert Reyes, panel discussion with Robert Crosby, NHCLC Latino Leaders Conference, Anaheim, CA, May 2016.

5. George, *Against the Wind,* 59.

6. Juana Bordas, *The Power of Latino Leadership: Culture, Inclusion, and Contribution* (San Francisco: Berrett-Koehler, 2013), 185.

7. Dr. Samuel Pagan, interview by Robert Crosby, September 6, 2016, Orlando, FL. Used by Permission.

8. Bordas, *Power of Latino Leadership,* xi.

9. Karina Ioffee, "Boom in Latino Evangelical Churches Underscores Growing Population," *Mercury News,* March 23, 2015, www.mercury news.com/2015/03/23/boom-in-latino-evangelical-churches-underscores -growing-population.

10. Pagan, interview by Robert Crosby.

11. "The Shifting Religious Identity of Latinos in the United States," Religion and Public Life, Pew Research Center, May 7, 2014, www.pew forum.org/2014/05/07/the-shifting-religious-identity-of-latinos-in-the -united-states, italics in the original.

12. Pew, "Shifting Religious Identity of Latinos."

13. Pew, "Shifting Religious Identity of Latinos."

14. Robert C. Crosby, "A New Kind of Pentecostal," *Christianity Today,* August 3, 2011, www.christianitytoday.com/ct/2011/august/newkind pentecostal.html.

15. Empowered21 is a collaborative organization whose mission is "helping shape the future of the Spirit-empowered movement throughout the world by focusing on crucial issues facing the movement and connecting

generations for intergenerational blessing and impartation." See www
.empowered21.com.

16. "Christianity in Its Global Context," Center for the Study of Global
Christianity, Gordon-Conwell Theological Seminary, June 2013, 54,
www.gordonconwell.edu/ockenga/research/documents/Christianityin
itsGlobalContext.pdf.

17. Ioffee, "Boom in Latino Evangelical Churches."

18. Pew, "Shifting Religious Identity of Latinos."

19. Bordas, *Power of Latino Leadership*, 185.

20. Joy Dawson, *The Fire of God* (Shippensburg, PA: Destiny Image, 2005),
12–13.

21. Robert Crosby, "The Church of Tomorrow," *Vital Magazine*, October
2014, 37–40, inaugural issue, https://issuu.com/vitalmagazine/docs
/vital_preview-issue_sm.

22. Barna: Hispanics, "Hispanic America: Faith, Values and Priorities,"
Barna Group, 2012, 4.

23. *Global Pentecostalism: The New Face of Christian Social Engagement*,
book summary, Amazon, www.amazon.com/Global-Pentecostalism-
Christian-Social-Engagement/dp/0520251946.

Chapter 3: The Third O

The chapter epigraph is taken from Sergio de la Mora, www.sergiodelamora
.com.

1. Jeff Shaara, *Rise to Rebellion: A Novel of the American Revolution* (New
York: Ballantine, 2001), xii.

2. Shaara, *Rise to Rebellion*, xii, ellipsis in the original.

3. A. W. Tozer, *The Pursuit of God* (Abbotsford, WI: Aneko, 2015), x–xi.

4. Dr. Samuel Pagan, panel discussion with Robert Crosby, NHCLC
Latino Leaders Conference, Anaheim, CA, May 21, 2016.

5. Juana Bordas, phone interview with Robert Crosby, October 19, 2016.

6. Robert J. House et al., *Culture, Leadership, and Organizations: The GLOBE Study of 62 Societies* (Thousand Oaks, CA: Sage, 2004).

7. Donald Miller, *Searching for God Knows What* (Nashville: Thomas Nelson, 2010), 204–5.

8. Elizabeth Dias, "Evangélicos!," *Time,* April 15, 2013, 3, http://content .time.com/time/subscriber/article/0,33009,2140207-3,00.html.

9. Tozer, *Pursuit of God,* 27.

10. Bianca Juarez Olthoff, *Play with Fire: Discovering Fierce Faith, Unquenchable Passion, and a Life-Giving God* (Grand Rapids, MI: Zondervan, 2016), 93.

11. Charles Spurgeon, "The Pentecostal Wind and Fire," *Spurgeon's Sermons Volume 27: 1881* (sermon 1619, Metropolitan Tabernacle, Newington, London, England, September 18, 1881), www.ccel.org/ccel/spurgeon /sermons27.xlv.html.

Chapter 4: The Pentecostal Paradox

The chapter epigraph is taken from Elizabeth Dias, "The Rise of Evangélicos," *Time,* April 4, 2013, http://nation.time.com/2013/04/04/the-rise-of -evangelicos.

1. Barna: Hispanics, "A Shifting Faith," Barna Group, http://hispanics .barna.org/a-shifting-faith.

2. Vinson Synan, *An Eyewitness Remembers the Century of the Holy Spirit* (Grand Rapids, MI: Chosen, 2010), 202–6.

3. Cary McMullen, "Holding Their Tongues," *Christianity Today,* September 21, 2009, www.christianitytoday.com/ct/2009/october/5.15.html.

4. See Donald E. Miller and Tetsunao Yamamori, *Global Pentecostalism: The New Face of Christian Social Engagement* (Los Angeles: University of California Press, 2007), 30.

5. Samuel Chadwick, *The Way to Pentecost* (Jawbone Digital, 2016), 89–90.

6. McMullen, "Holding Their Tongues," www.christianitytoday.com/ct /2009/october/5.15.html.

7. Rick Warren, address to the General Council of the Assemblies of God, Biennial National Meeting, 2011, http://agtv.ag.org/rick-warren-gc11.

8. Vinson Synan, "The Charismatic Renewal After Fifty Years," in *Spirit-Empowered Christianity in the 21st Century,* ed. Vinson Synan (Lake Mary, FL: Charisma House, 2011), 17–18.

9. David G. Roebuck and Darrin J. Rodgers, "Preserving and Sharing Our Heritage," in *Spirit-Empowered Christianity,* 229.

10. Harvey Cox, interview with Robert Crosby, March 17, 2015.

11. A. W. Tozer, *The Pursuit of God* (Abbotsford, WI: Aneko, 2015), 53–54, italics in the original.

Chapter 5: The Cries of a Community

1. Juana Bordas, *The Power of Latino Leadership: Culture, Inclusion, and Contribution* (San Francisco: Berrett-Koehler, 2013), 70.

2. Bianca Juarez Olthoff, *Play with Fire: Discovering Fierce Faith, Unquenchable Passion, and a Life-Giving God* (Grand Rapids, MI: Zondervan, 2016), 102–3.

3. Robert Crosby, "The Church of Tomorrow," *Vital Magazine,* October 2014, inaugural issue, https://issuu.com/vitalmagazine/docs/vital_preview-issue_sm.

4. Jens Manuel Krogstad and Gustavo López, "Roughly Half of Hispanics Have Experienced Discrimination," Fact Tank, Pew Research Center, June 29, 2016, www.pewresearch.org/fact-tank/2016/06/29/roughly-half-of-hispanics-have-experienced-discrimination.

5. Bordas, *Power of Latino Leadership,* 71–72.

6. Barna: Hispanics, "Hispanic America: Faith, Values and Priorities," Barna Group, 2012, 12.

7. Barna: Hispanics, "Hispanic America," 8.

8. "The Shifting Religious Identity of Latinos in the United States," Religion and Public Life, Pew Research Center, May 7, 2014, www.pewforum.org/2014/05/07/the-shifting-religious-identity-of-latinos-in-the-united-states.

9. Barna: Hispanics, "About Barna: Hispanics," Barna Group, http://hispanics.barna.org/about-barna-hispanics.

10. Barna: Hispanics, "A Shifting Faith," Barna Group, http://hispanics.barna.org/a-shifting-faith.

11. Justo González, *Mañana: Christian Theology from a Hispanic Perspective* (Nashville: Abingdon, 1990), 31.

12. González, *Mañana,* 32.

13. Jesse Miranda, panel discussion with Robert Crosby, NHCLC Latino Leaders Conference, Anaheim, CA, May 21, 2016.

14. Miranda, panel discussion, May 21, 2016.

15. Barna: Hispanics, "Hispanic America," 12.

16. Barna: Hispanics, "Hispanic America," 8–9.

17. "The New Colossus—Full Text," Statue of Liberty, National Monument, New York, National Park Service, www.nps.gov/stli/learn/historyculture/colossus.htm.

18. Gabe Lyons, phone interview with Robert Crosby, October 15, 2016.

Chapter 6: Introducing Billy Graham to MLK

The first two chapter epigraphs are taken from Trevor Freeze, "Remembering Dr. Martin Luther King Jr.," Billy Graham Evangelistic Association, January 15, 2017, https://billygraham.org/story/remembering-dr-martin-luther-king-jr. The third chapter epigraph is taken from Samuel Rodriguez, *The Lamb's Agenda: Why Jesus Is Calling You to a Life of Righteousness and Justice* (Nashville: Thomas Nelson, 2013), 75.

1. Edward Gilbreath, "History in the Making—Billy Graham Had a Dream," *Christian History* no. 47 (1995), www.christianhistoryinstitute.org/magazine/article/history-in-the-making-billy-graham-had-a-dream.

2. Scott S. Smith, "Thomas Paine's Writing Sparked American Revolution," *Investor's Business Daily,* July 1, 2013, www.investors.com/news/management/leaders-and-success/thomas-paine-advocated-full-american-independence.

3. See Samuel's book *The Lamb's Agenda*.

4. Robert Crosby, "A New Kind of Pentecostal," *Christianity Today,* August 3, 2011, www.christianitytoday.com/ct/2011/august/newkind pentecostal.html.

5. Deforest "Buster" Soaries, date unknown, Rochester, NY.

6. Donald Miller, "2006 SSSR Presidential Address—Progressive Pentecostals: The New Face of Christian Social Engagement," *Journal for the Scientific Study of Religion* 46, no. 4 (December 2007), 435, quoted in David D. Daniels III, "Future Issues in Social and Economic Justice," in *Spirit-Empowered Christianity in the 21st Century,* ed. Vinson Synan (Lake Mary, FL: Charisma House, 2011), 2.

7. Donald E. Miller and Tetsunao Yamamori, *Global Pentecostalism: The New Face of Christian Social Engagement* (Los Angeles: University of California Press, 2007), 339–40.

8. Miller and Yamamori, *Global Pentecostalism,* 123.

9. Elizabeth Dias, "Evangélicos!," *Time,* April 15, 2013, 4, http://content .time.com/time/subscriber/article/0,33009,2140207-4,00.html.

10. Dias, "Evangélicos!"

11. Crosby, "A New Kind of Pentecostal."

12. Freeze, "Remembering Dr. Martin Luther King Jr."

13. "The Road to New York City 1957," A Journey Through NYC Religions, video, 3:11, uploaded January 15, 2012, www.youtube.com/watch?v=2D xpUC5rNJg.

14. Sherri Jackson, "Franklin Graham Brings Father Billy's Legacy with Him to Birmingham, May 18, 2015, http://wiat.com/2015/05/17/franklin -graham-brings-father-billys-legacy-with-him-to-birmingham.

15. Billy Graham, *Just as I Am: The Autobiography of Billy Graham* (New York: HarperCollins Worldwide, 1997), 426.

16. "The Road to New York City 1957."

17. "The Road to New York City 1957."

18. "The Road to New York City 1957."

19. "The Road to New York City 1957."

20. Martin Luther King Jr., "Stride Towards Freedom" (address, Inter-American University, Puerto Rico, February 14, 1962), www.scribd .com/document/200921486/Martin-Luther-King-Jr-Speeches-in -Puerto-Rico-1962#fullscreen&from_embed.

21. Megan Briggs, "Martin Luther King Jr.'s Death Was 'One of the Greatest Shocks' of Billy Graham's Life," Church Leaders, January 16, 2017, http://churchleaders.com/pastors/videos-for-pastors/297 606-martin-luther-king-jr-s-death-one-greatest-shocks-billy-grahams -life.html.

22. "Taking Down the Rope of Segregation," video, 15:49, Billy Graham Evangelistic Association, January 18, 2015, https://billygraham.org /video/taking-down-the-ropes-of-segregation, at 2:40.

23. "Taking Down the Rope of Segregation," at 2:20 and 3:09.

Chapter 7: A Latino Pope?

The chapter epigraph is taken from Ann Schneible, "Don't Be Held Back: Pope Calls Christians to Be Set Ablaze by the Holy Spirit," *Catholic News Agency,* August 16, 2016, www.catholicnewsagency.com/news/dont-be-held-back-pope -calls-christians-to-be-set-ablaze-by-the-holy-spirit-85341.

1. Tamara Audi and Joseph de Avila, "Francis, the First Latin American Pope, Electrifies U.S. Hispanic Communities," *Wall Street Journal,* September 27, 2015, www.wsj.com/articles/francis-the-first-latin -american-pope-electrifies-u-s-hispanic-communities-1443389271.

2. Kaija DeWitt, "6 Fun Facts You May Not Know About Pope Francis," MSNBC, September 25, 2105, www.msnbc.com/msnbc/6-fun-facts -you-may-not-know-about-pope-francis.

3. Daniel H. Levine, "The Francis Effect," *America's Quarterly,* Fall 2014, www.americasquarterly.org/content/pope-francis-effect.

4. Daniel H. Levine, "The Francis Effect."

211

5. "Pope Francis Is Welcomed at the White House," Aleteia, September 23, 2015, http://aleteia.org/2015/09/23/pope-francis-is-welcomed-at-the-white-house.

6. "Pope Francis Is Welcomed."

7. "Francis to US Bishops: Speak with Everyone, Gently and Humbly," Aleteia, September 23, 2015, http://aleteia.org/2015/09/23/francis-to-us-bishops-speak-with-everyone-gently-and-humbly.

8. "Pope at 'Birthplace of America:' Defend Religious Liberty," September 26, 2015, Aleteia, http://aleteia.org/2015/09/26/pope-at-birthplace-of-america-defend-religious-liberty.

9. "Pope at 'Birthplace of America.'"

10. "Pope at 'Birthplace of America.'"

11. "Pope Francis Urges Faithful: 'Don't Let Your Hearts Become Numb!,'" Aleteia, September 23, 2015, http://aleteia.org/2015/09/23/pope-francis-urges-faithful-dont-let-your-hearts-become-numb.

12. Sarah Eekhoff Zylstra, "Pope Francis Apologizes for Pentecostal Persecution, but Italy's Evangelicals Remain Wary," Gleanings, *Christianity Today,* July 30, 2014, www.christianitytoday.com/gleanings/2014/july/pope-francis-apologizes-for-pentecostal-persecution-italy.html.

13. Zylstra, "Pope Francis Apologizes."

14. "The Shifting Religious Identity of Latinos in the United States," Religion and Public Life, Pew Research Center, May 7, 2014, www.pewforum.org/2014/05/07/the-shifting-religious-identity-of-latinos-in-the-united-states.

15. Priscilla Alvarez, "Can Pope Francis Reverse the Decline of Hispanic Catholics?," *Atlantic,* September 21, 2015, www.theatlantic.com/politics/archive/2015/09/can-pope-francis-reverse-the-decline-of-hispanic-catholics/406381.

16. Pew, "Shifting Religious Identity of Latinos."

17. Pew, "Shifting Religious Identity of Latinos." For the "17.6 percent in 2015" statistic, please see "FFF: Hispanic Heritage Month 2016," United States Census Bureau, release no. CB16-FF.16, October 12, 2016, www.census.gov/newsroom/facts-for-features/2016/cb16-ff16.html.

18. Pew, "Shifting Religious Identity of Latinos."

19. Elizabeth Dias, "Evangélicos!," 6, *Time,* April 4, 2013, http://content.time.com/time/subscriber/article/0,33009,2140207-6,00.html.

20. Dias, "Evangélicos!"

21. Howard Chua-Eoan, "Pope of the Americas," *Time,* March 13, 2013, http://world.time.com/2013/03/13/pope-of-the-americas/3.

Chapter 8: Race and Grace

The chapter epigraph is taken from J. Don George, *Against the Wind: Creating a Church of Diversity Through Authentic Love* (Springfield, MO: My Healthy Church, 2012), 28.

1. Dr. Samuel Pagan, interview by Robert Crosby, September 6, 2016, Orlando, Florida. Used by permission.

2. Alex Castellanos on *Meet the Press,* September 4, 2016, www.nbcnews.com/meet-the-press/meet-press-september-4-2016-n642656.

3. Gabe Lyons, phone interview with Robert Crosby, October 15, 2016.

4. Robert C. Crosby, "Gracelessness," *Patheos* (blog), May 30, 2012, www.patheos.com/blogs/robertcrosby/2012/05/gracelessness.

5. Stephen A. Nuno, "Here's How to Get the Latino Vote Right on Exit Polls," *NBC News,* November 21, 2016, www.nbcnews.com/news/latino/here-s-how-get-latino-vote-right-exit-polls-n684826.

6. "The Shifting Religious Identity of Latinos in the United States," Religion and Public Life, Pew Research Center, May 7, 2014, www.pewforum.org/2014/05/07/the-shifting-religious-identity-of-latinos-in-the-united-states.

7. Aaron Blake, "Obama's Immigration Executive Action Is Less Popular with Hispanics Than You Think," Washington Post, December 10, 2014, www.washingtonpost.com/news/the-fix/wp/2014/12/10/obamas -immigration-executive-action-is-less-popular-with-hispanics-than-you -think/?utm_term=.19774b28798b.

8. Jason Sowell, "Q Commons Event" talk, Oxford Exchange, Tampa, Florida, October 13, 2016. See http://qideas.org and http://oxford exchange.com.

Chapter 9: Answering the Prayer of Jesus

The chapter epigraph is taken from Lacrae, interview, "Q Commons Event" talk, Oxford Exchange, Tampa, Florida, October 13, 2016. See http://qideas. org and http://oxfordexchange.com.

1. Alexis de Tocqueville, *Democracy in America,* trans. and ed. Harvey C. Mansfield (Chicago: University of Chicago Press, 1985), paraphrased in Juana Bordas, *Salsa, Soul, and Spirit: Leadership for a Multicultural Age* (San Francisco: Berrett-Koehler, 2012), 37.

2. Robert D. Putnam, *Bowling Alone: The Collapse and Revival of American Community.* (New York: Simon and Schuster, 2000), 187.

3. Foner, *The Fiery Trial: Abraham Lincoln and American Slavery* (New York: Norton, 2010), 99–100, italics in the original.

4. Darrin J. Rodgers, "Assemblies of God 2014 Statistics Released, Reveals Ethnic Transformation," Flower Pentecostal Heritage Center, Assemblies of God, June 18, 2015, https://ifphc.wordpress.com/2015 /06/18/assemblies-of-god-2014-statistics-released-reveals-ethnic -transformation.

5. See www.mosaix.info.

6. Mark DeYmaz, *Leading a Healthy Multi-Ethnic Church: Seven Common Challenges and How to Overcome Them* (Grand Rapids, MI: Zondervan, 2010), 40–41.

Chapter 10: Beyond a Voting Bloc

The chapter epigraph is taken from Juana Bordas, *The Power of Latino Leadership: Culture, Inclusion, and Contribution* (San Francisco: Berrett-Koehler, 2013), 1.

1. Jens Manuel Krogstad, "Key Facts About the Latino Vote in 2016," Fact Tank, Pew Research Center, October 14, 2016, www.pewresearch.org /fact-tank/2016/10/14/key-facts-about-the-latino-vote-in-2016.

2. Bordas, *Power of Latino Leadership,* 47.

3. Marcela Valdes, "We're Looking at a New Divide Within the Hispanic Community," *New York Times,* November 15, 2016, www.nytimes .com/interactive/2016/11/20/magazine/donald-trumps-america-florida -latino-vote.html?_r=0.

4. Dr. Samuel Pagan, interview by Robert Crosby, September 6, 2016, Orlando, Florida. Used by permission.

5. Barna: Hispanics, "Hispanic America: Faith, Values and Priorities," Barna Group, 2012, 11.

6. Robert J. House et al., *Culture, Leadership, and Organizations: The GLOBE Study of 62 Societies* (Thousand Oaks, CA: Sage, 2004).

7. Barna: Hispanics, "Hispanic America," 10.

8. Barna: Hispanics, "Hispanic America," 9–10.

9. Bordas, *Power of Latino Leadership,* 1.

10. Nicole Akoukou Thompson, "Hispanic Consumers to Spend $1.3 trillion in 2015, Prompting National Economic Growth," *Latin Post,* 2015, www.latinpost.com/articles/82555/20150928/hispanic-consumers- will-spend-1-3-trillion-in-2015-prompting-overall-economic-growth.htm.

11. Hanna Rosin, "Did Christianity Cause the Crash?" *Atlantic,* December 2009, www.theatlantic.com/magazine/archive/2009/12/did-christianity -cause-the-crash/307764.

12. Tanvi Misra, "Immigrants Aren't Stealing American Jobs," *Atlantic,* October 21, 2015, www.theatlantic.com/politics/archive/2015/10 /immigrants-arent-stealing-american-jobs/433158.

13. Rainer Strack, "The Workforce Crisis of 2030—and How to Starting Solving It Now," TED, October 2014, www.ted.com/talks/rainer_strack_the_surprising_workforce_crisis_of_2030_and_how_to_start_solving_it_now.

14. Jeffrey S. Passel and D'Vera Cohn, "Size of U.S. Unauthorized Immigrant Workforce Stable After the Great Recession," Hispanic Trends, Pew Research Center, November 3, 2016, www.pewhispanic.org/2016/11/03/size-of-u-s-unauthorized-immigrant-workforce-stable-after-the-great-recession.

15. "Hispanics in the U.S. Fast Facts," CNN, www.cnn.com/2013/09/20/us/hispanics-in-the-u-s-.

16. Edwin Mouriño, "Awakening the 'Sleeping Giant': Latinos," Univision, November 7, 2016, www.univision.com/univision-news/opinion/awakening-the-sleeping-giant-latinos.

17. Jeffrey S. Passel and D'Vera Cohn, "U.S. Population Projections: 2005–2050," Hispanic Trends, Pew Research Center, February 11, 2008, www.pewhispanic.org/2008/02/11/us-population-projections-2005-2050.

18. Passel and Cohn, "U.S. Population Projections."

19. Janet Murguía, "Penny Wise, Pound Foolish? Don't Sacrifice Our Nation's Future," *Harvard Journal of Hispanic Policy* 23 (2011), www.questia.com/library/journal/1G1-288538012/penny-wise-pound-foolish-don-t-sacrifice-our-nation-s.

20. Elizabeth Dias, "Evangélicos!," *Time,* April 15, 2013, 6, http://content.time.com/time/subscriber/article/0,33009,2140207-6,00.html.

21. Bordas, *Power of Latino Leadership,* 46.

22. Bordas, *Power of Latino Leadership,* 46.

23. Bordas, *Power of Latino Leadership,* 154–55.

24. See Daniel Goleman, *Emotional Intelligence: Why It Can Matter More Than IQ* (New York: Bantam, 1995).

25. Pagan, interview by Robert Crosby.

26. Pagan, interview by Robert Crosby.

Chapter 11: Next-Gen Latinos

The chapter epigraph is taken from Juana Bordas, *The Power of Latino Leadership: Culture, Inclusion, and Contribution* (San Francisco: Berrett-Koehler, 2013), 16.

1. D'Vera Cohn, "It's Official: Minority Babies Are the Majority Among the Nation's Infants, but Only Just," Fact Tank, Pew Research Center, June 23, 2016, www.pewresearch.org/fact-tank/2016/06/23/its-official -minority-babies-are-the-majority-among-the-nations-infants-but-only -just.

2. Jens Manuel Krogstad and Richard Fry, "Dept. of Ed. Projects Public Schools Will Be 'Majority-Minority' This Fall," Fact Tank, Pew Research Center, August 18, 2014, www.pewresearch.org/fact-tank/2014/08/18 /u-s-public-schools-expected-to-be-majority-minority-starting-this-fall.

3. "New Census Bureau Report Analyzes U.S. Population Projections," US Census Bureau, release no. CB15-TPS.16, March 3, 2015, https://www .census.gov/newsroom/press-releases/2015/cb15-tps16.html.

4. Eileen Patten, "The Nation's Latino Population Is Defined by Its Youth," Hispanic Trends, Pew Research Center, April 20, 2016, www.pew hispanic.org/2016/04/20/the-nations-latino-population-is-defined -by-its-youth.

5. Barna: Hispanics, "Hispanic America: Faith, Values and Priorities," Barna Group, 2012, 10.

6. Stephanie Román, "Latino Millennials at Work, 2015: 5 Ways Employers Can Attract and Retain Latino Millennials," National Council of La Raza, June 30, 2015, 2, http://publications.nclr.org/bitstream/handle /123456789/994/millennial_employment_brief. pdf?sequence=1&isAllowed=y.

7. Juana Bordas, *Salsa, Soul, and Spirit: Leadership for a Multicultural Age* (San Francisco: Berrett-Koehler, 2012), 145.

8. Thom S. Rainer and Jess W. Rainer, *The Millennials: Connecting to America's Largest Generation* (Nashville, TN: B&H, 2011), 35–36.

9. Catherine Rampell, "More College Graduates Take Public Service Job," *New York Times,* March 1, 2011, www.nytimes.com/2011/03/02 /business/02graduates.html.

10. Douglass North, "Economic Performance through Time," *American Economic Review* 84, no. 3 (1994): 359–68, quoted in "Leadership in Latin America: Insights into Complexities Across Societies," Business Association of Latin American Studies, June 30, 2015, 4, www .balas.org/BALAS_2013_proceedings_data/data/documents/p639 350.pdf.

11. Patricia G. Martínez, "Paternalism as a Positive Form of Leadership in the Latin American Context: Leader Benevolence, Decision-Making Control and Human Resource Management Practices," in *Managing Human Resources in Latin America: An Agenda for International Leaders,* eds. Marta M. Elvira and Anabella Davila (New York: Routledge, 2005), quoted in "Leadership in Latin America," 4.

12. "Leadership in Latin America," 4.

13. Robert J. House et al., *Culture, Leadership, and Organizations: The GLOBE Study of 62 Societies* (Thousand Oaks, CA: Sage, 2004).

14. Román, "Latino Millennials at Work," 4.

15. Román, "Latino Millennials at Work," 4.

16. Román, "Latino Millennials at Work," 5.

17. "Hispanic Millennials: Top 5 Insights and Strategies," Latinum Network, www.latinumnetwork.com/hispanic-millennials-marketing -insights3, italics in the original.

18. Joel 3:14.

19. Román, "Latino Millennials at Work," 5.

20. Román, "Latino Millennials at Work," 5.

21. For more on teaming leadership, see http://teaminglife.com.

22. Bordas, *Power of Latino Leadership,* 206.

23. Rainer Strack, "The Workforce Crisis of 2030—and How to Starting Solving It Now," TED, October 2014, www.ted.com/talks/rainer

_strack_the_surprising_workforce_crisis_of_2030_and_how_to_start
_solving_it_now/transcript?language=en.

24. Dr. Samuel Pagan, interview by Robert Crosby, September 6, 2016, Orlando, Florida. Used by permission.

25. Barna: Hispanics, "Hispanic America: Faith, Values and Priorities," Barna Group, 2012, 10.

Chapter 12: Project 133

1. A. B. Simpson, quoted in Joy Dawson, *The Fire of God* (Shippensburg, PA: Destiny Image, 2005), 174.

2. Gastón Espinosa, *Latino Pentecostals in America: Faith and Politics in Action* (Cambridge, MA: Harvard University Press, 2014), 416.

3. Espinosa, *Latino Pentecostals in America*, 415.

4. Neil Rendall, "Moses a Tri-Cultural Man," InterVarsity Christian Fellowship, 2013, 4, http://mem.intervarsity.org/sites/mem/files /Moses%20A%20Tricultural%20Man%20Bible%20Study%20 -%20Complete%20Series_0.pdf.

5. Fanny Crosby, "Blessed Assurance," public domain.

Appendix

1. Mark DeYmaz, phone interview with Robert Crosby, August 30, 2016.

2. The multiple quotes from Bishop Harry Jackson come from a phone interview with Robert Crosby, October 28, 2016. See also www.the reconciledchurch.org.

3. J. Don George, *Against the Wind: Creating a Church of Diversity Through Authentic Love* (Springfield, MO: My Healthy Church, 2012), 28.

4. George, *Against the Wind*, 29.

5. George, *Against the Wind*, 30.

RESOURCES

These three organizations post the latest statistical information on Latino/Hispanic trends:

- Barna: Hispanics, http://hispanics.barna.org
- Center for the Study of Global Christianity at Gordon-Conwell Theological Seminary, www.gordonconwell.edu/ockenga/research /index.cfm
- Hispanic Trends at Pew Research Center, www.pewhispanic.org

FOLLOW, CONTACT, OR SCHEDULE AN EVENT WITH

Samuel Rodriguez, president of NHCLC

https://pastorsam.com

E-mail: info@pastorsam.com

FOLLOW, CONTACT, OR SCHEDULE AN EVENT WITH

TeamingLife
Enriching Circles of Collaboration

Robert Crosby, cofounder of Teaming Life

http://teaminglife.com

E-mail: info@teaminglife.com

Many teams find it difficult getting ahead due to conflicts and people differences. Teaming Life equips your organization to move from conflict management to *unity management* using our 7-Step Teaming Framework. That's when you will experience the best life—*the Teaming Life*—at home, work, church, and community.

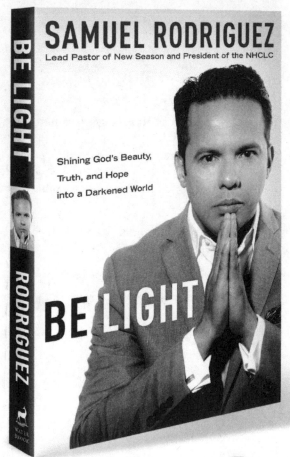